Stories £3.00
12/24
PJ.

NEW WRITING SC

NUMBER 7

NEW
WRITING
SCOTLAND
7

Edited by
EDWIN MORGAN
and
HAMISH WHYTE

Association for Scottish Literary Studies
with support from
Wm. Teacher & Sons Ltd

Published by the
Association for Scottish Literary Studies
c/o The Department of English, University of Aberdeen
Aberdeen AB9 2UB

First published 1989

ISBN 0 948877 06 5

The Association for Scottish Literary Studies acknowledges
with gratitude subsidy from the Scottish Arts Council
and the support of Wm. Teacher & Sons Ltd.
in the publication of this volume

Printed by AUP Aberdeen

CONTENTS

INTRODUCTION

Poetry, fiction and drama are all represented in this year's anthology — the last by a play for voices which could be either a radio drama or a piece of theatre in Beckett style. We continue the policy of mixing established and new writers, and we commend particularly some younger writers appearing here for the first time.

Some of the most interesting submissions we received, both in verse and prose, concerned 'the matter of Scotland', and it is clear that the present ruthless, half-hopeful, half-angry state of Scottish national affairs, whether political or economic or cultural, is now again finding literary, and indeed highly literate, expression. Nor is this at the expense of the local, as entries using different geographical areas of Scotland will testify.

Although we still receive too many nostalgic reminiscences, and too many conventionally celebratory poems about lochs and mountains, there was a refreshing variety of setting in this year's contributions: a BBC studio, a doctor's waiting room, a moth-invaded bedroom with a near-Hitchcock grue, a tiger's cage, a butcher's shop, an oil-rig core-sampling shed, a young man wearing his helmet at home after a motor-bike accident, the encyclopaedia-bay of a library, a field of aviators in 1910. It would be good to see more formal exploration, more risks being taken; and perhaps also more comedy and more satire. One brand of bad poem is depressingly prevalent: it comes trickling down the page in short lines, shapeless, rhythmless, devoid of pleasure to the ear, and frequently isolating in a line by itself some single word which is unable to bear that exposure and emphasis. These wilting, droopy pieces show, if it needed to be shown, that energy is the great desideratum in all creative writing, and fortunately we had no shortage of confident and vigorous submissions to restore the balance, and our spirits with it.

Edwin Morgan

Glasgow: June 1989

Hamish Whyte

NEW WRITING SCOTLAND 8

Submissions are invited for the eighth annual volume of *New Writing Scotland*, to be published in 1990, from writers resident in Scotland or Scots by birth or upbringing. Poetry, drama, short fiction or other creative prose may be submitted but not full-length plays or novels, though self-contained extracts are acceptable. The work must be neither previously published nor accepted for publication and may be in any of the languages of Scotland.

Submissions should be typed on one side of the paper only and the sheets secured at the top-left corner. Each individual work should be clearly marked with the author's name and address.

Submissions should be accompanied by two stamped addressed envelopes (one for a receipt, the other for return of MSS) and sent, by 31 January 1990, to:

Maggie Beveridge, Managing Editor *NWS*
c/o Language and Literature Dept
Mitchell Library
North Street
Glasgow G3 7DN

Balfour Brown

A FRENCH TUNE

On the trip to the BBC the taxi-driver was affable, but his words were too rapid and Glasgow for her to understand. After a gear change, he spoke loudly and slowly as to the deaf, 'We have a lot of visitors because of the Festival.' She found stilted speech catching, 'Unfortunately I am only here for a short time.'

On Great Western Road near a scaffolded building she said, 'I have not been here for ten years.' (It was nearer twenty.) 'There have been many changes.'

Looking sly, the driver said, 'Plus ça change . . . . N'est-ce pas?' He laughed.

So the tune had stuck. She smiled ironically instead of saying, 'I'm not French.' Till 3 a.m. in a corner of her hotel bedroom she had listened to herself speak lines from a script. Every word had to have its normal English pronunciation; only the tune of the phrases and sentences was to suggest French. The learning and unlearning had been exhausting.

Her cassette recorder was in Cheltenham.

They were approaching a bridge and she clutched the brown envelope that held the script. She didn't want to enter Broadcasting House far too early.

'Could you let me off at a corner? I've forgotten something. Please.'

As she stooped, opposite an Art Deco building, to pay the driver, his face became Glasgow sardonic and she wondered if he would attempt some French farewell.

'Okeydoke, hen. Have a nice day.'

She had glimpsed from the taxi a shop called Wheelcraft with mottled pots in its window. She began to walk towards this too far to reach, stoneware destination.

The autumn breeze thinned her tweed suit. Her reflection in the window of a bank said that being attractive, like being comfortably off, was only a limited consolation. At an Indian gift shop she saw — behind elephants, salad bowls, inlaid boxes — silk squares in colour harmonies she liked.

'If you'd wrap these two. I'll wear this.'

The Indian had a pepper-and-salt beard. While she tied the scarf in a cravat, he assisted with a carved hand-mirror. 'That is very good. Very nice with your jersey. Very suitable for . . . actress.'

For a moment she thought he might, long ago, have seen her on the stage. Then she saw the envelope she had laid on the counter.

'Many people come here from BBC. News people. Music people. But you are actress. I can tell.'

She wondered if he could tell that she was afraid.

'You have some very nice things.'

'Thank you. Please come again. Always new things coming in.'

The Indian hadn't thought she was French. The hotel bedroom came to her — in an echoing corner the found tune, the lost meaning. I dislike James Cafferty intensely, she told herself. Tugging at the shop door, she conceded, Not dislike. Fear.

You weren't afraid of Tyrone Guthrie, she reasoned, why should you be afraid of James Cafferty?

There were shadowy passers-by, decently dressed, some with shopping-bags. A dentist's brass plate put doctors in her mind. Valium, she half-believed, could shield her from the ordeal of Cafferty.

'You do not need valium,' said Dr Aleb the Cheltenham wonder doctor, 'you need to look in the mirror.'

She stopped at the bridge above unspectacular water. Across a bridge of twenty years she was in the theatre, the heroine of Schiller's *Maria Stuart*. Today she was Mary Queen of Scots, in a radio play by an antiquarian journalist.

A young man was shouting to another, 'I dunno. I'll maybe not manage on the Tuesday.' She repeated the strange locution, giving it a French tune.

On the narrow street which yesterday's taxi had used the houses were small, Georgian, reserved. The script was swinging out of time with her footsteps and she tucked it under her arm. A blackbird flapped up from a garden, seeming autumnal. From a house with uneven blinds she heard a muted Hoover.

A blackbird rose slowly at the back of her mind as a forgotten symbol. Not from a play. Perhaps a poem. Or an advertisement.

The BBC loomed like a school or a hospital, and the script reflected her heartbeat. She knew that these upper windows were the windows of producers' offices. No, she told herself, that's silly — no Cafferty is malevolently staring down on you. She fingered her scarf.

Iron gates. Sloping tarmac. Cinema doors. In the foyer a schoolboy with a Greek motto on his blazer was chewing gum. She needn't approach the elderly receptionists. The rubber-floored corridors were bleakly clean. She wouldn't take the slow lift to the third floor.

She climbed up, wishing she were climbing down.

The drama block was on a split level, approached by its own terrace of stairs from whose lower half the waiting area was out of vision. The waiting area, which seemed to be called the Drama Lounge, was a carpeted corridor, lit by steel-framed windows and furnished with settees and chairs. So early, she hoped there would be no one or only a stray technician.

The relief of emptiness. Then she saw that, half-hidden by the most distant settee, someone was sitting, crouched or huddled, on a tubular chair. She recognised him as a sickly young man who had a few lines as a servant. She regretted not knowing his name.

'Hullo,' she said. 'Are we the first?'

'Morning.' The young man began to stand up, then sat down again. He was clutching a magazine. 'Probably in the canteen.'

She translated this as, Other early birds having a coffee. The magazine was *Amateur Photographer*.

'Is the lift broken, that it's so slow?'

'I think it's for pianos.'

She pretended to look out of one of the windows. The view was of roofs, ventilators and blank sky. She declined to discuss the weather. The man opened his magazine.

'Are you a photographer?'

'No. It was lying here.' He found a handkerchief. 'Would you like to see it?'

'No, thank you. I think ... ' She began to retreat. 'I think I'll just go into the studio ... Perhaps ... '

She meant Studio 8, which, used only for Mary's soliloquies, she regarded as her own. She could have meant Studio 4 where she interacted with the rest of the cast. 'I'll just go into my studio' sounded vain.

She stopped in her studio's sound-proofing vestibule, the size of a telephone kiosk, and fumbled the script from its envelope. She could murmur her lines here, safe from an eavesdropping microphone.

The acoustic was different from that of the hotel bed-room, and the tune sounded flat and false. She tried again. In judgement of her conscientious Cheltenham study Cafferty had said, 'Let's get rid of all the zeezat stuff. We can do with-out the French equivalent of Mummerset. That's absolutely unacceptable.' When she said, 'I'll tone it down,' he answered, 'No, it's detestable. Reform it altogether.'

Muttering between vestibule doors felt foolish and illicit. Anyway it was overkill.

Retrieving the envelope from the carpet was a kind of grovelling.

The muffled dusty electronic smell of the studio dis-turbed her nerves. Her table had rounded corners and a can-vas surface. She opened her handbag and sat on a springy chrome chair to calm herself with new and old treasures — scarves, compact, keys, scent, pen ... She laid the tissue-paper parcel on the canvas, to unwrap slowly, to unfold. The microphone was a sinister high-tech épergne.

If she said — as was true, 'I'd find things easier with a stand-mic instead of a table-mic,' what contemptuous or im-patient response would come from Cafferty?

He had despised her from the first cold handshake. In all this time he had not once addressed her by her name.

She inferred from scattered hints that she wasn't his choice but had been wished on him by higher authority. She also sensed that as a Roman Catholic he found it offensive that a Protestant actress should play so Roman Catholic a queen.

She could stand contempt or hatred. What was humiliating was the fear.

She laid out two scarves like tea-cloths. Some of the prints were misregistered and she didn't know whether this was a merit or a defect. She remembered a TV rehearsal in a Croydon church hall where, on the wooden floor, the colours from a stained-glass window were broken by strips of coloured Sellotape.

The monitor speaker came alive with a breath of white noise, then died with a click. She thought the mic might now be live and drew her scarves away from it. The sweep seconds hand of the studio clock didn't sweep, but jerked jarringly a centimetre a second.

In the Drama Lounge the actor playing Cecil rose from rummaging in his briefcase and role-played the courteous host. He was dressed as for the golf course and had on his little finger an amethyst ring. When she was beside him, uncomfortably, on the settee, he revived the harmless conversation of the previous day. She achieved a bright manner.

'I do love the Cotswolds,' Cecil was saying, when she heard the lift gates and a clatter of people. Like a consultant in a teaching hospital, Cafferty and his subservient entourage slowly ascended into the lounge. She smoothed the script on her knee. While the actors settled, Cafferty, shadowed by his female secretary, paced to the far end of the room and became preoccupied.

She stared at her script, aware that although he had changed his shirt he was grimly identical with what she remembered. She disliked the sharp-elbowed lumberjack shirt and the corduroys whose seat his bottom was too thin to fill. She disliked his unwashed-looking iron-grey hair. She feared his face, emaciated by resentment. He could smile with his voice but not with his mouth.

He stood near her, waiting like a schoolmaster for attention. His secretary was at his elbow, holding up his clipboarded script. 'Well, folks . . . ' His deep voice was casual but his shoulders were tensely raised.

Assisted by his secretary, he was skimming through the script to deal with points left over from the previous rehearsal. He would pace to the actor concerned and, stooping impatiently, hand down his instructions, then retrace his steps. 'Bill . . . ' When he had a note for Cecil she stared downwards, aware of his thin wrists and of his belt buckle. ' . . . On page four. Not so irascible.' He paced away from her neighbour's grateful response. Distance was a respite. She had monologues on pages five and six.

He seemed, so that no one should feel unvalued, to be going to raise a hurried point with every member of the cast. In suspense she turned pages to wherever he was at. He commended the servant. It occurred to her that he might, then she was certain that he would, exclude her from these attentions. A non-person, she tried to joke. A coldness spread through her.

In theory she could refuse to be ignored. She could assert herself by saying, 'Could I possibly have a different microphone?' She dared not.

'Let's shamble through then . . . Let's say, from seven minutes to . . . '

She wished she felt anger, not unworthiness.

Her scarves and their wrapping lay on the table like an

unappreciated present. She folded them slowly and carefully
to show them they were valued. They weighed almost nothing.
The tandem cue lights flicked on and off, she believed in
error, but she coughed in case they were enquiring if she was
there. She wouldn't be needed for at least five minutes.

The springy chair was never at an optimal distance from
the table. She was comfortable neither sitting upright nor
leaning forward. Her forearms on the table-top felt heavy and
incapable of gesture. Denied a stand-mic, she was thankful
for the small mercy of not having to wear headphones. The
script lay open at her first page. She knew most of the words
by heart.

From the monitor, which would go silent thirty seconds
before her cue, hushed breathings and rustlings diminished.
Seven minutes to. Music. Dialogue. Hold ups. Cafferty, deeply
patient, very finicky. The actors — they would be old acquaint-
ances — relaxed.

As her part drew nearer, the hand of the clock jerked
more violently. Her scarf was too tightly tied. When the
monitor went dead, the clock hand jerked inside her. Fixating
the script and the table cue light, she inhaled too early.

Always expecting Cafferty's intervention and always in a
state of fear, she couldn't perform. But her voice could.
Automatically it began, without Mummerset, and went on,
apparently controlled. Separated from her voice, she felt un-
real. The passage came to an end.

' . . . Right,' said Cafferty wearily. ' . . . A moment.'

There was a suspense of white noise.

At last Cafferty said, 'To cue music, the last three sentences again. In your own time . . . '

She had to have some recognition of her transformed
French. 'Mr Cafferty . . . ' She couldn't solicit an acknow-
ledgement. ' . . . Am I to begin without a cue light?'

'Just in your own time.' He interpreted her longing. 'I
said Right, didn't I? Comparatively speaking it's all right.'

'There's usually a temporary cue.'

' . . . We're economical here.'

She saw the contemptuous implication — economical
with praise. No bouquets.

'Sorry. I'll go on a count of ten.'

She silently counted, then began four, not three sentences from the end. She wondered defiantly if he would say,
'Can't you count?'

The next scene began, and she had four pages' rest. But it

was all right, if only comparatively speaking. The 'here' of
'We're economical here' took on meanings. Glasgow. Was
there a chip-on-the-shoulder contrast with London? Did
Cafferty think she thought she was a metropolitan slumming
among provincials? She searched her memory for anything
derogatory she might have said — about weather, the hotel,
transport, the slow lift ... Or when she expressed pleasure,
was that taken as condescension?

'You see demons,' said Dr Aleb, 'where no demons exist.
That is why you run away and hide.'

She was thankful she was hidden from Cafferty.

The acting coming through the monitor from Studio 4
seemed phoney. She banned judgement in case criticising
others brought misfortune on herself. She traced the typed
words with a finger.

Control, control, control, she told herself. For this passage have control.

'Script noise,' accused Cafferty.

Her script lay on the canvas table-top absolutely silent.

' ... Sorry,' she said.

'Script noise destoys any possible illusion you might
achieve.'

' ... I'll try to watch it.'

She began again. 'Wait for the cue light.' She waited and
the twin light pulsated an angry green Morse as if she were
late.

Uninterrupted, she did find more control. By the end of
the passage she found some of the stilted words pleasurable.

' ... Better, I thought. Before, that was probably your
worst page.'

'Thank you.' She didn't know why that particular page
had been conspicuous for badness. Indecisive script noises
from Cafferty.

'I may be getting used to it. Give me the last page again.'

'From the top?'

'In your own time.'

It was a hard sentence to begin on cold. He didn't let her
complete it. 'You're saying "beciz". The word is because. Be-
cawz.'

'Oh. Mummerset. Sorry.'

'Not vaudeville French, no. An affectation. It's an English
actress affectation, to say "beciz".'

'I'll watch it.' She altered the spelling to becAWse.

'From. The. Top.'

Habit defeated the phonetic spelling.

'Mark it on your script, will you. I don't think you see how appalling it is. A contemporary English affectation. We're supposed to be sixteenth century. Did you know that when Mary wasn't speaking French she spoke in Scots?'

'Oh ... '

'No, we don't want Scots. There's historical fact and there's dramatic expectation ... Can we go again.'

She negotiated because, and played thoughtfully.

'Too aware of the audience. It's not a Schools broadcast.'

She was aware of the audience in Studio 4, monitoring her failures. 'Sorry. I didn't notice. Less pointed.' Then he might accuse her of lack of thought. 'It's difficult to know how far to go. When the language is so archaic.'

'Often from the *Essay on Adversity*. Often the words of Mary Queen of Scots herself.'

A translation, she silently retorted. Mary wrote in French.

'Often her actual words.'

' ... I'll work on it.'

'It's not a technique thing. It's an absence of imaginative identification. The give-away is your complaining about archaic language. Until it becomes your language, there's no empathy with the character.' He had a fit of coughing and it made his voice harsh. 'I don't know about you, but for me the whole justification of the play as radio is the quality of Mary Stuart's meditations. That's what demands real acting. Not the big speeches at the trial. Any stick could do them.'

As well as faulting her monologues, he was belittling her past success in Schiller.

'That, incidentally, is the wherefore of the table-mic. Because Mary would be seated. Does that suit?'

The one chance of saying, No, please, I'd be happier with a stand-mic.

'Yes,' she said. 'Thank you.'

Her script was pencilled in magnified writing: Go to 4 for page 14.

In Studio 4, which had NO SMOKING signs, she met again — most of them seated, bored — Mary's adversaries: Paulet with cigarette and in jeans, Walsingham with bow-tie and cigar, double-breasted Bromley, golfer Cecil ... All strangers to her, all sycophants of Cafferty. Two actors were declaiming to a microphone behind black screens. The photographer servant silently offered her a chair and she smiled and shook her head.

Her episode with the jailer Paulet was a hollow victory. She was genuinely impassioned, but any stick could have done it.

The monitor in the Drama Lounge could summon her, if there were any notes, to the too smoky studio. She went to the end of the lounge farthest from the cliff of stairs. The steel-framed windows were sealed. The doors near her were those of effects studios, with grams and stone and gravel footsteps. She picked up *Amateur Photographer* from the carpet and put it on the arm of a settee.

She was looking at the grey sky above roof and ventilators and half-expecting a blackbird to appear, when her right shoulder sensed danger. She turned her head and saw far away arising from the steps Cafferty. Her courage drained. She stared at a ventilator.

She realised that his business could not be with her. But as he came nearer she felt physical fear as if he were going to strike her. He hurried past, causing a movement of the air, into an effects studio.

Her heart slowed and she could run away. Dr Aleb smiled. The window glass didn't reflect her face.

What should she say to Cafferty? The most she could say would be 'Hullo.'

She waited with the script in her hand as if it were the X-ray of a shameful illness.

If only either could manage a smile.

When the door opened on his leanness and greyness and checked shirt, she couldn't pretend anything. His face came into focus. He looked tired. His eyes had an emptiness, the opposite of a smile.

'Yes,' he said, and walked away.

You didn't exactly meet him half-way, she joked as she hurried back to her studio. Well, anyway, I didn't run away. Reason couldn't exorcise fear.

The dusty electronic smell was now scented like the hotel bedroom. Awareness of lack of sleep depressed her.

She sat at the restrictive table and, listening to the monitor, found the place in the script. She turned to her next scene to search for and respell becauses. There were none. She turned back to her cue. She disliked Scotland. She stroked her scarf. In a way scarves were futile.

The monitor was silent and she was lost. The cue lights demanded and she hadn't an answer.

'Anyone in Eight?' He never gave her her name.

'Yes. Sorry ... Is there a cut?'

'Yes, there's a cut.'

'I'm sorry, Mr Cafferty. I haven't one marked.'

'In the lounge, this morning, I gave it.'

'May I have it now.'

With weary distinctness as to someone very stupid he spelled out the cut in the script. Making heavy pencil obliterations, she was thankful her own part was still intact. She took cuts personally as if they were the surgery of her failures.

'Thanks. Sorry about that.'

Her heart was beating faster, not from fear but from an impotent resentment. In the Drama Lounge Cafferty hadn't informed the assembled company of any cut in the script. He must have given this cut individually to the particular actors involved in the scene. Treating her as a non-person, he'd forgotten that the cut would affect her cue.

Or had he forgotten? Could he have planned this embarrassment?

She was looking for non-existent devils. She must, as with the accusation of script noise, rise above unjust blame.

'Just when you're ready.'

Ironically, the next speech was about Mary's determination not to weaken. It still seemed too stiffly literary to be heartfelt.

Saying 'abhorred and horrid slough of pusillanimity', she shortened the last word to 'pusillamity'. She tried again, and distorted the word to 'pusillaminity'.

'Pu. Sill. An. Im. Ity.'

'Pu-sill-an-im-ity. Yes. Sorry.'

She acted again and stumbled on the word.

'It's Mary's word. It's as if she doesn't know her own name.'

'Pusillanimity.'

'It means cowardice.'

She began the speech and he cut her off at 'abhorred — '

'No. Scrub it.' In the hotel the polysyllable had flowed naturally. 'Put "cravenness".'

' "Abhorred and horrid slough of cravenness"?'

The monitor didn't reply. When she had written CRAVENNESS on the script, she found that her hand was shaking.

'Cravenness' was easily said.

But the repetition of 'r' in 'abhorred and horrid slough of

cravenness' betrayed her into using the French trill of the previous day. She came to a stop.

'Is your score marked "canzicrans"?'

'What?'

'Because, like a crab, you are going backwards.'

The whiteness of the page glared and the lines of print went out of alignment.

'I'll get it right this time.'

The monitor was blackly silent.

The lines of print swayed like snakes and words went in and out of focus. But she knew them by heart.

The page might go blank and her memory might go blank.

If she stopped and couldn't go on, she would claim a migraine. Or, I had a migraine in the night and it's come back a little — it'll soon go. She must keep Cafferty out of her studio. Without his physical presence all fear was manageable.

Her voice was subdued and deaf. She heard it murmur in non-vaudeville French, 'abhorred and horrid slough of cravenness, an evil place which those called on by God to rule must shun.' Legibility settled on the perilous page. Towards the end she became aware of, and tried to recover from monotony.

She took off her scarf and waited. From the monitor came the slow sound of turning pages which seemed made of wood. Her neck felt prepared for execution.

'It's gone the other way. The other extreme.'

'Yes, I saw that. Flat. Not pointed enough.'

'Pallor and inwardness, yes. Suffocated vitality, no.'

' . . . I'll work on it.'

The sleepless hotel.

'It needs an imaginative leap.'

So that archaic unnatural speech becomes natural speech with a French tune. Speech not spoken but thought and felt. Speech that Mary looked like. Speech that Mary was.

' . . . Yes.'

The boom and tear of a struck match. Cafferty's cigarette not white but iron-grey.

'I think I see . . . I think — I'm sure — tomorrow you'll see a difference.'

'I'm glad to hear it.' Wooden pages. ' . . . Bill . . . David . . . '

'Yes, Jimmy?'

He never addressed her by name. He had three days till Goodbye to give her once her name.

By tomorrow the promised transformation couldn't be complete. 'I thought we were to suffer a sea-change.' Not yet. Soon. In the end.

Sleepless persistence for whose sake? Hers? Cafferty's? The journalist's? Mary Stuart's? Everybody's? Hers.

'You are obsessive,' said Dr Aleb. 'All artists are obsessive.'

On her next page, where Mary was ill, she had printed NOT HUSKY. She scored out the instruction. She doodled the outline of a bird and filled it in black.

Not yet, but in the end.

And then?

Then an irreconcilable handshake, without her name, 'Well, thank you again.' And fear, hurrying her to a taxi. 'Goodbye, Mr Cafferty.' No vestige of a French tune. 'Goodbye, I've enjoyed it.'

Elizabeth Burns

THE LAIRD'S WIFE VISITS THE POORHOUSE

she brings me roses
pink and fullblown ones
tight-budded white ones
does she think I can eat
these sweet petals?
will the sight of them
fill my stomach?
what colour are a bunch of flowers
in this peat-smoked
one-candled cupboard
of a room?
can their scent
drown out its stench?
roses
and here each inch
of land taken up with
potatoes   turnip   barley
a rose bush?
it would be pulled up
by its thorny branches
the earth dug greedily
planted with food
and she —
and she —
her ladyship —
I will strip the petals
from these flowers
with my teeth
chew them up
spit the bitter pulp
and woody stems
onto the fire
burn them as fuel
that they might have some use
and may their smoke

choke her as she walks away
may the perfume of her garden
that she tells us is so famous
turn sour as burning flesh
and may her pink and white skin
be stripped from her bones
and spat to herring gulls

I bury my face
in bitter roses
and begin to bite

Stewart Conn

AT *LES COLLETTES*

i

Scarcely any distance from the peopled *plages*
extending their pebbled curve to Menton
and beyond, under the broiling Mediterranean sun,
leave the boulevarde and climb by the Passage Renoir
to *Les Collettes*, built for my final years.

In the hour before the house opens for the afternoon,
stroll round the gardens, under those knotted olives,
themselves a vast age before we came to occupy the place.
Shade your eyes, as I had to, and look across
the chasm of light between here and the château

at Cagnes. Imagine me, being wheeled down
these paths in my wooden chair, or sitting hunched
over that day's canvas, in my open-air studio.
Then enter the house, and experience (as I did)
its coolness. Go up (as I could not, latterly, unaided)

to the *atelier* on the first floor, and look down
as I constantly did, on the powdery green
of the olive-trees. Consider them, if you care,
with their gnarled contortions, a metaphor
for my deformed hands' durability, through pain.

ii

Fortunately I had too much to keep me busy,
to worry about Cézanne and Matisse and the others
changing the face of Art. As I gather
turned out the case. I always kept to a sole design;
whereas they saw from several vantage points, at once.

Not only that, but they'd detect angles and prisms
in their subjects, where I'd see only smoothness.
I sometimes wondered what chaos it could lead to —
especially when that dark-eyed young fellow Picasso
(born the year I did my *'Déjeuner des Canotiers'*)

came bounding, like a goat, on the scene,
promising to go further even than their extremes;
painting what he *thinks*, not what he sees.
One clear reason why, rather than contemplate
the future, I was happy to remain in the present.

For all that I admit (in trust) to a desperation
that once what is new has been superseded
by the 'new' new, my early work, derided
at the time, may be seen in fairer perspective —
and it be conceded I opened shutters, let light in.

iii

Sleep comes over me. I have been too much in the sun.
And begin to be overtaken by some kind of delirium.
Purveyor of order, resident in this rectilinear mansion,
so meticulously terraced, I see myself as at times
contributing a geometry of my own; a peripatetic sundial

round which revolve fragrances, qualities
of brightness and shade, which I must transmute
to paint, transforming their colour temperature.
A process easy to attribute to sheer *joie de vivre* —
if only to put the culture hounds off the scent.

They never comprehended, for instance, how Aline
dictated her own style. Not least, through my delight
in her rotundity: midway between fantasy
and reality. More splendidly too, than with any
other model, her skin responded to the light.

Even that, now a secondary consideration.
I miss her so much. Above all, the softness
of her fingers, as she wound the bandages on.
This, in my retentive memory, the one thing
that dulls the pain. I wish she were with me again.

MONFLANQUIN

We follow the track to Monflanquin,
on either side the sheen of rippling grain,
past the churchyard with its flaked stone

and flowers preserved under bell-jars.
As we stand there, a coach drawn by white horses
glides past. Is that the music of the spheres

we hear — and is it too part of a fantasy,
like the shimmering pantiles, the sky
too blue to be real? Try though we may,

it is difficult in such an atmosphere
to remember we are no longer
the definitive selves we once were.

Such timelessness cannot last.
This holiday must not go to waste
or become a thing of the past,

but remain part of what we share,
absorbed by our love for one another
so that having returned together

to our customary and more mundane
surroundings and diurnal routine,
within ourselves we jealously retain

those moments by that honey-coloured château
where we stood arm in arm, as from an upper window
came soaring the overture to *The Marriage of Figaro.*

MANZÙ EXHIBITION: LAST AFTERNOON

Do I see you through his eyes or my own,
fragile girl poised on the rim of a chair
too high for you? For what house-party or play
were you dressing up? Such haughtiness of expression,
mouth turned down at the corners, eyes
with a Japanese slant, you seem simultaneously

come-hitherish and shy, as if saying, 'Capture
I defy you, the evanescence of this moment':
which is precisely what the sculptor has done.
Closing time approaches. Uniformed attendants
unhinge wooden shutters. Footsteps click
on the polished floor, as hushed visitors,

ourselves among them, scurry for a last glimpse
of a favourite piece — with in the centre room
that slouched Cardinal, dominant as on a throne.
Reverberant doors slam. Rather than imagine
the sculptures imprisoned in darkness,
alone, I sense the pervading presence

of an elderly man in an accustomed jacket
and soft hat; hands, unable to dissimulate,
kneading clay like dough: so intense
the humanity with which he imbues
his figures, they resonate in the memory —
incomparable bronzes, lubricated by light.

Robert Crawford

DIALOGUE

In the trailer-park two trailers are drawn up back to back, each coupled to a lorry cab. A single polished wooden chair sits on the end of each trailer. The chairs face one another. The two friends

sit on the chairs and start talking about the state of their country, remembering their childhoods, and hopes there had been then of a remedy. Sometimes the two friends

agree, sometimes they differ strongly. As they share a packet of biscuits, solutions emerge, a plan of action. Then the lorries rev up, move off. A widening gap appears between the chairs, but the two friends

stay seated, go on talking, though by now one lorry is winding into the northern uplands, the other accelerating far south. The two friends

speak simultaneously, often brilliantly. Occasionally messengers in cars drive at high speed from one to the other with tapes and shorthand transcriptions but the conversation remains out of sync, however much the two friends

do not want it to be so. This was a long time ago. Now there are only two empty chairs (one in a north-east fishing village, the other in a southern pedestrian precinct) facing each other. When people see either chair they walk forward to read the inscription. Each chair is called *The Two Friends.*

PIMPERNEL

Maybe it was a woman who escaped,
Aged about thirty, joking
She had hair that grew like a hedge.

She mentioned to nobody she was the one.
She turned down the graduate scholarship
Once held by Adam Smith.

Beautiful feet. Her job brought her circulars
Urging the enhancement of macromanagement
For the information resource.

When that language
Made her cry, was it fair
To say yes, it's written like shite?

Nowhere to go, she's the escapee
Who one night rolls over towards you
In bed in a country that hasn't existed

For centuries, whispering, 'I've become a nationalist.'
You can't advise her, now she's your wife,
You listen to her, writing the poems.

PUNSS

Ah felt a swivvle o wund swoich oot
Blawin a gumphion past
Alang thi seaters an owre thi streets
Til it claucht me fae sleep at last

But Ah jist turnd owre an poyned oan a dream
Tae fleg awa yon hairms:
Ah'd pook'd an rook'd aa America
An Ah held yi, punss, in ma airms.

UNEXPLAINED

I felt a strong wind that sweeps round a corner whistle
hollowly out, blowing a funeral banner past along the
meadows and over the streets till at last it suddenly seized me
from sleep

but I just turned over and worked diligently and anxiously
on a dream to scare away these harms: I had pillaged all
America and I held you, unexplained, in my arms.

ROOM O THI LOOF

Aneath yon lither we plout-net fur thi time
That's cummin tae slee in, thi time whan we'll mak
Wurds' puddock-hair gang packlie, an loo skyre oot
Its yule-blinker fund in thi yarkins.

Rainie o yir rails, rinrigs o breists in thi daurk.
Awa yi slabbers, yi daft teevoos!
Ther's aye wan room ushed an kept gey lounlie
Fur thi naikit huzziebaw o nicht.

ROOM OF THE PALM OF THE HAND

Beneath that yielding sky with undulating clouds, using a
small stocking-shaped net and two poles, we search for the
time that's coming to slip free in, the time when we'll make
the unfledged down of words work intimately, and love shine
out clearly its north star discovered in the side seams of a
shoe.

Continual repetition of your bodices, stratagems of breasts in
the dark. Away you slovenly people, you stupid flirting men!
There's always one room cleared and kept absolutely protected
from the wind for the naked lullaby of night.

TRANSFORMER

Lengths of model railway track jutted from the Pictish stones.
When I bent down to look at a horseman's head or at the
comb and mirror, scale-model engines hurtled towards me.
Ivanhoe, The Lady of the Lake, The Fair Maid of Perth with
gleaming pistons -- I had to catch them or they'd shoot off
the ends of their tracks. I lurched from stone to stone, grab-
bing them. In the darkness they slackened off. At midnight
I wrapped the locomotives in plastic bags to carry them
away; their metal bodies grew heavy and cold as I walked.
Home, I laid them in the loft, peering at them, wondering if
they'd work on my layout. That night I saw them carved
new, crewed by warriors, steaming their way into battle. At
Aberlemno model replica carriages with Victorian coachwork
lay in the grass, unspotted. Mist was perforated by cries and
grinding metal. *Royal Scots* poured from the stones.

Leslie Crook

POEMS

A night breeze on a calm sea lulled Palinurus to close his eyes
Rest now said Phorbas in a dream the following wind will do
    your work

The prow cut through moonlit mist and Sleep dropped from
    the stars
He caught himself gripped the helm held the course set
    through shadows

Sleep wiped a bough dipped in Lethe over the leading
    steersman's eyes
He fell headfirst into the waves and the cold water woke him

The oarsmen slept on the hard benches none heard sinless
    Palinurus call
Stones growled on the shore where the surf was a whispered
    voice

Finally trusting the sky and the sea he died without a shroud
The fleet drifted on past the drowning son of Iasus

Love is as simple as breathing you say
Asthmatic in love cowed before the
Effort of climax I agree
The rain-spattered struggle misted window
Hides the world from us or us from the world
If it's not a contest why do I feel I have lost
The opened door lets in cold street
Strangers pass our bed on the way to the shops

Eighty cold nights I loved a happy bachelor
Wrapped my legs round him and pulled
My cracked lips sometimes mutter his name
And I remember our grapples
I remember what we did to each other

The first notes were for you my favourite rival
Where are you now to listen to my pastoral

When alternate voices struck the delighted air
Heifers forgot to eat puzzled lynxes cocked their ears

The brooks paused frozen by your sweet melodies
Will the hour come to praise your tragedies

When night was slowly fading from the sky
I asked the morning star to bring a kind day

Take this this poem written at your request
Round the laurel on your brow ivy to twist

John Cunningham

THE AVIATORS

On winter evenings he fed the cows after the milking, pushing between them with armfuls of hay. They were tethered to the stalls loosely by chains round their necks but he had to mind the points of the horns as they turned with their soft eyes, sweet breath and rasping tongues curled delicately out for the hay.

It was 1910 and Howard was a year older than the century. They had the small farm of Burnfoot where they grew oats and potatoes, reared a few sheep and the cows on whom they mainly depended.

In the mornings he helped his mother and father with the milking; when the milk was cooled it went into the big metal churns. The cows, about a dozen depending on how many had calved at the time, gave enough milk to fill three churns a day, and they were taken to the Creamery in Lanark.

On Saturdays and in the holidays it might be Howard who took them, in a cart pulled by a big white bony horse. Ever since he'd been old enough to do this there had been days when an aeroplane droned over like a wasp, low because it would be going to land at the Racecourse; he would see the man's head and might get a wave of his leather-gauntleted hand, but he didn't wave back. The aviators weren't ordinary people; their photographs were in the paper sometimes. They belonged in papers. He got on with the job, thinking his own thoughts and watching the backside of the horse and hearing the heavy chinking of the churns.

If he went by the top road he'd sometimes see the planes on the Racecourse, though never going up or coming down, as if they did that in secret.

'They're asking for trouble,' his father said, his big legs folded at the table, the tackets in his boots squealing shortly when he moved — ready to stride out if anything was wrong — his moustache bristling over the paper. 'They'll catch it,' he'd add. In the early days of aviation his father detested its uselessness and looked for the flyers to get their come-uppance.

And being superstitious as well as Christian he was certain they'd get it that very year, the year of Halley's Comet. But when the clear May nights came and they saw the Comet passing over, no disasters had struck the Lanark flyers. The world went on as usual; other people joked about the old notion that the Comet brought bad luck. In the farmhouse his father went on insisting they'd get their deserts sooner or later — because they flew in the air, boldly challenging the stars Howard supposed, although he felt that his father was dead set against them for more reasons than that.

On Saturday 11 August they staged an international competition with contestants from England, France and the United States. Coming back the Racecourse way from the Creamery, he saw planes of every colour in front of the grandstand. Going among them were the aviators, shouting and laughing. He stopped the cart. They were ordinary people, but different from anyone he'd met in Lanark. He remembered a group of bicyclists he'd met on the road once, men and women in strange clothes. They'd greeted him as they passed, friendly but entirely different. He'd stared without answering but days later was excited to have been, it seemed, equals on the road. The aviators were something similar ... he trotted the horse home, the empty churns bouncing in the cart, and said he was going back up the road for brambles.

His father looked at the sweating horse, and after a pause he said that that would be alright. Howard could see he knew the berries were red yet, like the ones behind the steading that they always picked; and he understood that this was a lesson being set up for him when he came home without brambles: not to tell lies. And there'd be another lesson behind this one, the real lesson: that his father had been right about that sort of new-fangled nonsense coming to grief.

With so much against him he forgot it all and slipped through the Racecourse fence.

A crowd mobbed around the grandstand where they served drinks and sandwiches. He made his way through the high society of Lanark, dolled up to the nines and mingled with noisy, alarming foreigners. He wished he hadn't come. Then as no-one paid any attention to him, he wandered out among the planes. They were fragile and dazzling, the opposites of the solid farm carts. Sometimes the aviator would be sitting in the cockpit while a mechanic tried the plane's propellor. In others the mechanics tuned the engines. The air was full of roaring, the strange exciting smell of gasoline, and drawling voices talking of their kites.

He found himself beside a yellow plane. A man in the cockpit, in ordinary cap and glasses, looked straight at him through the thick lenses. 'Hey, will you lend me a hand?' he called in a kind voice. His plane was as yellow as scrambled eggs.

Howard hesitated. 'Yes,' he said at last.

The man asked him to hold a bolt on the outside while he tightened the nut inside the fuselage. It was done in a moment. 'That's it!' he shouted cheerily when it was fixed.

'I hope you win,' Howard said.

'Thanks, my boy!' shouted the aviator above the roar of the engines, 'Keep your fingers crossed for me! Number 24!'

There was shouting through a loudspeaker, increased roaring of the engines, throbbing of planes, a movement of the crowd to get the best places on the rails, people running in their fashionable clothes. He ran too, dodging through them to the blackboard beside the grandstand. He read: '24 — Mr Cecil Grace — Farman monoplane.'

The heavy, powerful roar of engines increased though it had already seemed as loud as it could be; the planes rolled at intervals across the turf and took off as lightly as flies.

24! Still wearing cap and glasses as if he was going for a walk, he lined up for his turn. You could see it was just pure fun for him. He waved — to someone special it seemed — and moved to the start of his take-off. Howard was anxious. This man might be the target of his father's prediction and the Comet's bad luck. He was too happy.

The yellow plane wafted up as if carried by a gust of air and circled higher and higher among the rest. The sky was full of planes like birds, circling and getting smaller. Howard was dizzy from looking up. He couldn't tell which was number 24 any more, they were too high, but the yellow plane was in his thoughts so much that he feared to see it falling from the sky, twisting and spinning.

He felt the fear in his legs and ran from the Racecourse.

No-one asked where he'd been. His father didn't mention brambles. Howard feared that he could make a crash happen by willing it, and couldn't get out of his mind the picture of the yellow plane tumbling downward. He went about his evening jobs in torment, and it was the same at the morning milking. He dressed for Church expecting the minister to announce a crash from the pulpit and use it for a sermon — while he was trapped in the pew. But the service passed without a mention of aviation — as if it hadn't happened — and there was not a word about the competition outside after, when they were standing around chatting. If there'd been an accident, there would have been!

The paper carried the result later in the week. Monsieur Drexel had won in his Bleriot monoplane, setting a world record of 6,750 feet. Mr Grace had been fifth. He was alright! And now Howard saw him distinctly when he'd landed, handing over his kite to the mechanic, smiling, moving in a slow easy way, short-sighted in the glasses.

There had been no accidents at all. He began thinking that his father could be wrong — a gradual process; the thought had been in his mind some time before he acknowledged it. He grew used to it then, but as a single instance, not affecting the rest of his father's enormous rightness.

In November, a mild November that wouldn't harm a fly, not the wild windy sort, an aviator made a solo flight from France to England, lost his way in the fog and disappeared. From the position of the bits of wreckage he seemed to have wandered too far north-east. It was feared, from the various objects recovered, that the pilot had been Mr Cecil Grace, the distinguished flyer. And later it was confirmed that Mr Grace had indeed left France that morning. Unless he had been miraculously picked up by a fishing boat, this brought the deaths by flying accidents for the year to the melancholy total of thirty. Was it not time to ask ourselves, etc., etc. . . . The paper had been left for him to see.

The Comet! And *he* had attracted its attention to Mr Grace, by being there, connecting them in his mind. He'd been led there all the same, with the small lie about the brambles, and he hadn't been able to stop, entangling himself and Mr Grace both, by creeping through the fence, then going out away from the crowd, speaking to the man, a stranger after all. He shouldn't have looked at him, never mind answering his question, should have kept walking. And Mr Grace, whose fingers had tightened the nut through the fuselage from his, was dead. He cried, afraid of being found, and went out to the byre, hid behind the pile of hay in the corner and cried more but without relief. His mother found him and he wouldn't say what was the matter for a long time, and then he couldn't explain anything to her, except that Mr Grace was dead.

As time went on he understood from the way his parents talked to him that it was not right to mope for a long time,

for a stranger and that one especially, and as the days passed
he hid his sorrow. Days and months covered it. He'd never
known someone who'd died; he wandered about the fields
on his own, thinking he was going to get a spar or strut from
the wreckage by some miraculous means; in the evening, with
the atlas under pretence of geography, he studied again the
best route to walk to the English Channel.

Cecil Grace (he'd dropped the Mr — blushing in the dark
the first time) had taken the final place, the favoured one, in
his prayers. Was it right for someone dead? Should it have
been his soul to be blessed? No, the real Cecil Grace must be
blessed every day, to keep him as he'd been in the aeroplane
the first time he'd looked through those glasses and called
out for help tightening the bolt.

Perhaps CG — he began to call him — mightn't need his
prayers now he was up there man to man with Jesus, there
was no way of finding out, but he went on *in case* they were
needed; also it was his best way of keeping in touch.

He began talking to the cows again as he pushed between
them, and just about then his voice broke.

Elspeth Davie

DEATH OF A DOCTOR

The doctor's nursing-assistant comes into the waiting-room rather earlier than usual — just before seven o'clock, in order to say a few words to each person sitting there. The room is already half-full. It is midwinter, and throats and chest complaints can be expected. Even though the place is warm enough some people are still wearing scarves. The children have on their knitted woollen caps.

The girl standing in the doorway is an extremely pretty person. In spite of her stiff white cap and the well-laundered blue overall there is nothing starchy about her. She hesitates for a moment on the threshold, looking about her, then begins to go round the room, saying something quietly to each patient. The words, in fact, are so quiet they can scarcely be heard except by the one person she is speaking to. What she says is, 'I am very, very sorry. I have to tell you that Dr Sneddon died last night.' Often she gives a little touch to a shoulder or to a hand as she says this, and occasionally a light tap on a head as if to instil some unbelievable message into the hard skull as gently but firmly as possible.

Snow is beginning to fall, though the flakes are still so few they can hardly be seen except when they fly suddenly sideways and glitter close to the waiting-room window. Sometimes they are blown backwards and up towards the high wall of the house opposite. This long, black building has lighted windows in it and now and then a dark figure can be seen — a woman at a sink, an old man pulling a sweater over his head, a dim room behind, sometimes a set table, and always from the corner the flickering blue light of the TV.

'Dead?' says an elderly man to the assistant. 'Oh, but I've been here a long, long time, and I've come a very long way too. I had to leave my work early. And that wasn't easy, I can tell you.'

This waiting-room is by no means a gloomy place. It could almost be called gay with its brightly coloured posters stuck on every inch of the wall — posters about Accidents in

the Home, about Diet, about Drink and Driving and about
Exercise — showing swimmers, runners, walkers and people
bending and stretching in airy bedrooms. There are posters
asking for Kidney Donors, Eye Donors and Blood Donors.
There are new posters about AIDS and well-known ones
calculated to reduce the fear of cancer. There are posters to
encourage Cervical Check-ups and discourage Smoking. There
are posters on Contraceptives and Healthy Motherhood, on
Pre-natal Clinics and Post-natal Clinics, on Childcare, on
Vaccination and Immunisation. Some of these posters make
a dramatic pictorial impact with their flaming frying pans and
dizzy drivers steering toward the crash, by their enormously
fat and attractively slim people, their mothers with perfect
babies and mothers with sad babies. The frenzied business-
men with bulging eyeballs, heading for the heart attack are
hung beside careless people cutting themselves with sharp
instruments, or poisoning themselves with badly-labelled
bottles. Yet whatever these poster-people are doing they are
still managing to hang onto life, if only by their fingernails.
The elderly man scans them all carefully and seems to feel
the lack of something. 'Well, I've been here since six,' he says
again as if this fact in itself should awaken the dead. He stares
fixedly at the door as though awaiting a resurrection.

'Yes, I know,' says the girl patiently. She has heard often
enough what people can utter under shock. 'And another
doctor will be coming tomorrow,' she adds. Yet the man
doesn't look shocked, simply tired — tired to death you
could say.

'Well, *when* is the other coming?' he calls after her as she
moves on to speak to three people, a young girl in a red coat
with her child, her father and mother, the child's grand-
parents, on either side of her.

'How can that be?' says the girl almost brightly when she
hears. 'I saw him two days ago. He looked flourishing. Said
he'd been golfing. The best round he'd ever had, he told me.'

'You've got to expect anything,' says her father. 'I, for
one, am *ready* for anything. That's how I've always gone
through life.'

'Well, that's absolute nonsense,' says his wife. 'You're not
ready for anything — never have been as long as I've known
you. You were never ready when the builders came, never
ready for the plumber, always late with the TV licence. When
were you ever ready for visitors, even your own grandchildren?
How can you be ready for death?'

'It's all beyond her, poor thing,' says the old man, appealing to the nurse with a friendly smile. 'She's speaking of death as a person, isn't she? She's not into the big ideas yet, you see, not into the abstractions.'

But the young nursing-assistant goes on quickly to take her message round the room. Two pregnant women sitting together take it very badly indeed. Both weep when they hear it, knowing very well how birth and death can be spoken about in the same breath. For a moment the nurse sits between them and puts an arm round their shoulders, praises their hair, their eyes, their complexion, speaks of the happiness of new life, compares their choice of babies' names, asks after the other children and reassures them about the other doctor who will be coming in tomorrow. 'But is he as good, as kind?' they ask anxiously, their hands laid protectively on their bellies as though round precious, easily-damaged jars.

There is now a feeling in the room, even amongst those who haven't heard, that something has gone wrong with this place tonight. Several persons get up and slowly approach the table where daily and weekly papers are laid out along with certain magazines — Romance, Beauty, Housekeeping for women, Gardening, Fishing, Engineering and Do-it-yourself for men. People are taking a long time to choose. There is a great deal of fussing, rustling and whispering round the table. The women leaf impatiently through those pages devoted to polishes and perfumes for the face and body, polishes and perfumes for the house. Some of the magazines are fearfully old and limp, rough-skinned and dingy. Yet some glamour still remains. Unlike the recent dailies no tragedy has touched them. Both men and women pick up these newspapers very cautiously tonight, glancing back and forth from the pages to the white-flecked blackness beyond the window as if forcing themselves to relate the innocent white-on-black outside with the sombre, headlines black-on-white within.

The young assistant leaves the pregnant women and continues on her round. Those who suspect nothing out of the ordinary watch her coming gratefully. She is indeed young and pretty, unlike a harbinger of death. On the other hand it seems just possible that she is coming to tell them some comforting news she has picked up about their ailment. Unlikely but possible. In this building all possible and impossible things have been heard and spoken. 'Well, when *is* the other one coming in?' shouts the elderly man from the other end of the room. In the silence following a man holding a fishing magazine

is heard to remark that fishing has saved him. 'Not drugs,' he
says, 'not doctors, not diet, not exercise.'

'What was wrong with you then?' says the man beside
him. 'What was wrong, that only fishing helped?'

'Nothing wrong with the body,' says the other. 'Not unless you can talk of a body as strung with nerves as a hung-
up puppet. Nerves were what was wrong. Nerves and nothing
else.'

'Sounds bad,' says the one beside him. 'I've never had
that. But what have fish got to do with it?'

'Casting a rod over a deep pool is what it is. Flicking the
fly over a flowing stream. Not a sound from the bushes on a
still day and not a ripple on the pool. The one and only thing
that's cured a bad bout of nerves. No, don't talk to me about
the medicine men, don't give me the psychiatrists. This is
Nature, you understand. Or maybe you don't. Not many do
these days.'

'But there's the tooth-and-claw bit, of course,' says the
one beside him. 'How do you square that?'

'I don't. I've seen creatures gobbling one another up
while I sat peacefully on the bank, insects biting, tangling to
the death with other insects, great bugs chewing up small
bugs. I've seen cats purring and pawing over mice, grown men
forcing poison down rabbit holes. Screams and agony all
around on a summer's day.'

'Funny that doesn't get on your nerves,' says the other.

'Well, I count myself one of these animals, of course.
Maybe that's the reason. I've got used to my own cruel breed,
for better or worse. I'm pretty tough, I daresay. Though I admit I came round this evening because I didn't feel so good.'

Having got through papers and magazines there is little
for the patients to do except watch the girl making the round
of the room. Everyone stares at her — the women even more
than the men. Their feelings are mixed. Some who have been
flicking through Romantic Stories ask themselves whether
the doctor has ever been in love with her. They wonder what
the lonely, ageing wives make of such girls — the beautiful
attendants of doctors and dentists, the glamorous private sec-
retaries of business executives and politicians, the gorgeous
guardian angels of every clergyman, spiritual director, and
bishop, the comely companions of all-night petrol pump
attendants, the stunning policewomen and the teacher's
pretty helpmate. Tonight the thought of this weakens their
resistance more than the flu or the sore throat, more even

than the asthma. The awful injustice of it all grabs them in the pit of the stomach like the start of labour pains. True enough, somebody said the wife is everything at the end of the day. A faithful wife is more precious than rubies. Rubies, was it, or was it emeralds? Emeralds or diamonds or just plain pearls? It is always terribly hard to get these jewel qualities of wives properly sorted out.

'And when is the *other* coming?' shouts the old man again from the end of the room.

'Just hold your tongue, you, and show some respect!' a woman exclaims.

Some of the children are getting bored now. There are a few toys near the table but they are for the younger ones. The older group ignore the scarlet wagon on wheels, the drum, the yellow truck carrying bricks, the moth-eaten teddy bear. The tired babies, their eyelids a faint blue with sleepiness, have started to wail and are being bounced on their mothers' knees. The girl in the blue overall watches the older children for a while, then holding a small boy and girl by the hand she takes them to the window and lets them kneel, each on a chair, to watch the flakes blowing outside. Now more people can be seen peering from kitchens across the street. Some there have almost forgotten they are looking into a waiting-room. They have stayed so long staring out from darkening, empty rooms, it seems they are envying the carefree closeness of the crowd opposite — the lively talk, the table covered with papers and coloured journals, the toys, the children playing, and in their midst this amiable young woman who is exceedingly attentive, who bends and speaks intimately to each person in turn like the good hostess at a party. The food is lacking, certainly, but no doubt there is a laden table somewhere behind the scenes.

By this time the nursing assistant has reached a very old man sitting close to the gas fire. He is holding a small sporting paper and his hand shakes so wildly the sound of paper is out of all proportion to the size of page. It resembles some gale-swept poster tearing itself off the sea wall. His head is shaking too. To those who watch, it looks as if he is not at all startled by the girl's message, but rather affirming every word she says with a violent nodding of the head as if — unlike the others — he is agreeing silently but energetically that death is inevitable, not surprising at all and must be continually accepted without question. The girl braces his shoulders firmly for a second and passes on to a youngish couple sitting

together by the window. 'Will he be long over the patients tonight, do you think?' says the woman glancing over her
shoulder. 'We've such a distance to get home. If this goes on
we might even be stuck out there. This time last year the car
scarcely got through the last two miles on the hill. Of course,
I know he can't help it. But will he be long? My husband's in
pain. It actually took him an age to get down into this chair.
He can neither sit down nor stand up, you see. And as for
lying! Even a few pills for the night would help. Of course
the doctor can't help it. He's no say over his time when the
surgery's full. That's the worst of practices these days.'

The young assistant is thoughtful for a moment as if considering carefully this question of time. She raises her eyes
and looks into a mirror between two posters on the opposite
wall — one persuading people to stop smoking, the other dis-
creetly mentioning kidney donation. 'No, they'll never get a
kidney out of me,' says the grandfather of the child as he
follows the direction of the girl's eyes. 'Not a kidney, not an
eye! I'm keeping every bit of myself to the grave, and every
drop of blood to the last. It's hard enough keeping myself
together as it is, and getting harder and harder every day!'

In the mirror the girl's face looks smooth and youthful.
To the old people it seems she could never be thinking of the
passing of time, far less about death. Still she conscientiously
gives her news to the once snow-bound couple who lean forward attentively to listen, then grab one another's hands.
This young husband who is supposed to be unable either to
sit down or stand up, gets to his feet in one straight, sudden
movement like a dancer who raises his partner with him by
force of an unexpected discord in the musical score. The
three of them stand together for a moment — the young
couple with the nurse. Slowly she presses them down into
their chairs again. She takes great care doing this — putting
one hand on the woman's shoulder, supporting the man's
back with the other and making sure their feet are firmly set
on the floor — planting them, so it seems, like fragile plants
into deep earth before she turns away.

Beside them are two men discussing the repair of an old
car. The older has his arm encased in plaster from wrist to
elbow and he holds it out stiffly in a half-salute towards the
middle of the room. Once in a while children come up and
tap it curiously with a fingernail. Unlike the drum on the
table it makes a dull, heavy sound. These men have already
heard what has been said to the couple on their right. The

nurse stops beside them only for a moment. 'Well, that's
the saddest thing,' says the younger man, 'and he can't have
been much older than me. I always liked that doctor — loved
isn't too strong a word. He came once in the middle of the
night — when I could hardly breathe, when I was in such a
panic I thought it was the finish of me. Believe it or not, I
started to breathe again the minute that man came through
the door. And when he started to talk to me things were OK
as if nothing had happened. What did he talk about? I remember something about his mother's hens. Anyway the
sheer stupidity of those hens, clucking and scraping through
that night, brought me round. And then the smooth, harmless eggs lying there in the morning straw. Well, the whole
thing calmed me. Whenever I have another attack I think of
hens. What else he did for me I *can't* remember. The poor
young man. To tell you the truth I'm terrified to hear the
news. I feel bereft. I'm sorry I sound so heartless — talking
about myself,' he says to the nurse.

'Not heartless at all,' she replies, noticing that he is pale
and beginning to gasp a little like a man forcing his head
suddenly out of a strong wave. She takes his hand and draws
a deep breath. When his colour returns and they are both
breathing slowly and regularly together, she moves on. Once
again from the far corner of the room the old man shouts
louder than ever, 'When is the other *coming*?'

It is snowing heavily now, and with their fingers the
children follow the criss-crossing tracks down the window-
pane or make sudden, swooping movements with their hands
as the flakes blow upwards on a gust of wind. In the windows
of the houses opposite several persons are still staring across.
Some have even left the TV screen to watch. The ghostly
blue light still flickers behind them as they peer enviously
down into this real, lit room full of flesh and blood men,
women and children with their genuine fire, their real toys,
papers and pictures and all presided over by a friendly girl,
prettier than a TV star. This girl has made the full circle of
the room and now she reaches the door where she stands in
silence. Everyone waits for her to speak, even the children
loading the yellow truck with the last brick and the kneeling
snowflake-tracers who have now climbed down and are rub-
bing their red knees. The watchers in the windows opposite,
seeing nothing but her moving lips, wonder if she is welcoming the company, promising better to come, or already on the
point of saying goodbye. 'I am so sorry I had to give you this

news tonight,' says the girl. 'It's a terrible shock for all of us. You've waited here too long, I know. But I thought it better to tell each one of you.' She puts her hand on the door and tells them that another doctor will be here early the next day and that meantime any emergency can be seen round the corner in the next street. She gives a name, a street number, a telephone number. And now she waits for the patients to leave. Slowly they get up, one by one, and come across. Some touch her quickly on the arm, in passing, or on the shoulder, as she has done to them. One or two give the crown of her head a quick light stroke. These are all cautious touches as if to discover if she is truly flesh, blood and bone, to make sure she will still be there for them tomorrow and the day after and all the weeks to come, if need be. Yet all these discreet touches have done something to the girl. Her hard, shore-substance is being gradually dissolved by this sea of need. The determination is wavering slightly. The last persons to leave see that she is in tears.

In spite of the movement through the door the waiting-room is not yet empty. An old woman, sitting where she has sat for the last half hour, is still there, knitting. Opposite, on the other side of the table, a serious middle-aged man is still engrossed in his book. Long ago the nurse has spoken to them, but it is as if they had never heard. She approaches the woman. 'The others are going now,' she says. 'I'm afraid you'll have to go off as well. You see, I have to close the place in a few minutes.' For a while the knitting needles click on more rapidly than ever. Then the old woman drops the red, woollen scarf for an instant to remark, 'I am waiting to see my doctor! No, not *any* doctor. My *own* doctor! Even if I have to wait all night!'

'Will you help me?' says the girl, moving across to the reading man. 'She doesn't seem to know what's happened, though I tried to tell her. Perhaps you can help. I'm sure you understand.'

'Yes, I understand all right, but I can't help,' says the man. 'Of course I'd *like* to help. But I can never get this death business into my head straight off. I don't just mean the doctor's death. Any death. It's stupid, isn't it? At my age. Utterly stupid and childish. But do you mind if I sit here for a while longer till I get the hang of it? Then I'll certainly try to persuade the old girl to leave with me. Do you mind?'

'No, I don't mind at all,' says the girl, 'and I'll sit on myself for a bit. There's not all that hurry.' The three of them sit silently and apart with only the sound of the needles clicking and the surreptitious turning of the pages of a book. After a while the girl goes through a door leading to a cup- board and comes out five minutes later with a tray, a pot of tea, three cups and saucers, sugar, milk, three biscuits on a plate. She pours the tea and hands it round.

Opposite the lonely TV watchers, peering from dark rooms through flurries of snow, can scarcely believe their eyes. Oh, the luck of some people! This easy get-together, the comfortable tea-talk and the friendly warmth on a freezing night. How they have missed all this, not just this night, but every night! Yes, every night of their lives this very thing has managed to go past them without their knowing it.

The man with the book makes the first move. He goes across to the old woman and takes her ball of wool between his hands. 'What's this you're knitting?' he asks. 'A scarf for my third grandchild,' she replies. 'Two years old next month.'

The man presses the soft, scarlet ball against his cheek and stares at her. 'Will you let me take you home in my car?' he says. 'I'm going to take the young lady home too. So you'll be perfectly safe,' he adds.

'Yes, I'll go,' she replies. 'Though I'd always feel perfectly safe here, of course, even if I was the last one left. As a matter of fact I always feel safe when I'm waiting to see the doctor, though I do happen to know there are certain folk who feel they've never been nearer danger or even death when they set foot inside this waiting-room. But there's really no need for that, is there?'

'None at all,' says the man. 'Come along now before it gets worse out there.' He takes her one arm, the girl takes the other, and they leave the room.

The snow is driving down so thickly against the windows that, fortunately, no watcher from the opposite side can now see this desolate, vacant room, its empty chairs arranged like some seance which — deserted by all its members — still hopefully awaits the return of one punctual and devoted spirit.

G.F. Dutton

Lachie

the roof lasted
a little longer than he did.
they sold his sheep, the beasts

went to the knackers, the tractor almost
too rusted
to move. he lived on

in drink and conversation,
guffaws, a hundred
tales of wit

and prowess fading slowly,
as the place itself had foundered
into one more green

nettle-making heap but that
an architect bought it,
for weekend use,

with a professional wife
three small children
and a dog called Simon. Saturdays,

from the hill the house
smokes at evening again,
fresh-painted, with a new straight roof.

they sold his sheep, the beasts
went to the knackers, the tractor almost
too difficult to move.

docken

and there is a docken
that each year
grows hugely in a corner
of the carpark, that has seen

three factories take on this site
and has outlived
all three, survived to be
just now Japanese, it is

a great favourite,
old Willie Stout
the gardener does not dare
spray it or howk it out.

a tall docken
with a long stem
that rises from
the secret to the sun.

the concrete garden

it takes time
to become set. before that

you spread it out
smack it, thrust

bright-eyed advances
about the agglomerate, sow

whatever is new,
bound to grow,

push through,
rise to you there — you

regarding from heaven
before the streets stiffen.

even then, they swear, one mushroom
can break up a pavement.

death in October

good to go off in colours.
scarlet before the sleet,
fuming crimson, shrieking orange
a relaxed butter-pat

yellow. name them. anything
is better than flat
worn out green. even that
is strangely remote

in frost lying on the white
grass, whiter
edged, each vein
picked out for the last time, crystalline.

Gerrie Fellows

EFFIGIES

They delve into cubic rubble   tunnellers
of particularity   burrowing
through the multitudinous dusts of brick
ash   the skin's microscopic scales

Touching at last   beyond a chair's straight
back   an elbow crooked in a sleeve
A child and a woman as they were at a table
together when the dust met them
(meeting itself   could go no further)

The house closed over them   choked every opening
took each hand upon the table   their arms
her breasts beneath the porous woollen shirt
Laid itself heavily over the bright kerchief
Embalmed the boy's ink curls

The searchers' hands uncover them   clothed
for winter mid-morning   They might be
plaster casts in their blanket of ruin
Even the chalk loaf she was about to slice
with the sand knife

The rescuers bring oxygen
(It spills before them in a flood)
They bring light to the dead

But the dead   (who are their own effigies)
have no need of it

Sandy Fenton

GLORY HOLE

Gweed kens fa pit it in — ah weel, no, gweed kens an' I ken,
an' it wisna me, bit gin I tellt ye, some een mith get tae hear
o't, an' syne 'ere'd be ower mony maisters, as 'e taid said till
'e harra. Weel, there wis nae dogs an' nae cats aboot 'e hoose,
an' nae ither kin's o' beas' tae ait it, an' ye couldna mak'
porrich or brose wi't — nae unless ye wis ready tae pick caff
oot o' yer chowdlers for 'e rest o' 'e day. I niver speert far it
cam fae, bit intill 'e glory hole it geed, a plastic baggie o' bran
that mith ay 'a' come in handy for something.

It 'id been 'ere a lang time. A glory hole's nae a place ye
min' tae keep snod. If ye're needin' something oot o' 'e road,
in it goes, an' gey lucky if ony reddin up's deen eence a 'ear.
Files I've gotten scunnert masel an' I've teen oot 'e ironin'
byeurd, siveral pairs o' sheen, boxes 'it hid been teemt bit
niver trampit on an' tied up for 'e scaffie, newspapers — God!
newspapers, Scotsmans, wik-eyn Observers, a fyow aal Sunday Times, a pucklie People's Journals and People's Freen's
'at hid got wachlet doon fae 'e Northeast, Sunday Expresses
'at 'e dother brocht roon fin she cam for 'er Sunday denner
an' didna ay min' tae tak awa again, colour supplements,
wifies' papers 'at tellt ye aa aboot Charles an' Diane an' geed
ye yer horoscope as weel's 'e latest cure for breist cancer,
nae tae spik o' heapies o' cut-oot re-sipes an' squaars o' faalt-
oot sweetie papers an' choclit wrappins' — tinnies o' pint an' a
baldie-heidit brush 'at no't a new wig, teem biscuit tins 'at
some o' 'e trock kidda been stappit intil, twa coal shovels in
'perfeck condeetion' as 'ey say in 'e adverts, twa or three
great big boxes o' Ariel washin' pooder, een o' 'em half skailt
ower 'e bit o' aal linoleum 'at didna richt cover 'e fleer, fire
irons on a cowpit imitation brass stand o' best weddin' present quality, a plastic pyock full o' plastic pyocks, an', aye, bit
'e best bittie o' aa, 'at wis 'e nyeuk I'd teen ower masel. I'd
gotten haad o' a timmer box, pat dowel rods intil't, up an'
doon an' across, an' made a fine rackie for 'e wine I bocht be
'e dizzen bottles fae ma freen Roddy, gettin' a bittie off for
bulk buyin'. I likit 'e fite wines mair'n 'e reed, bit nae aabody

his 'e same tastes so I ay tried tae cater for ither fowk tee.

Ah, weel, eence aathing wis oot 'ere wis a kinna teem stewy smell — funny, doon by here 'e fowk wid say 'stoory', or raither 'stooray' — bit I niver likit tae spile 'e wye I wis brocht up tae spik. I ken 'e wird 'stoory' fine bit ye winna get me sayin't. An' I winna say, 'It'll no dae' fin I've aye said 'it winna dee'. 'E queer bittie o't is, it's ither wyes o' spikkin in ma ain country I'd raither nae folla, though I scutter on fine wi' ither fowks' languages. Even aifter gettin' in 'e lang spoot o' 'e Hoover, ye'd ay get that stewy kinna atmosphere, so naething for't bit tae pit aathing back in again, or maistly aathing.

Though I used 'e glory hole for ma wine cellar it wisna a' that caal. Een o' yon nicht-storage heaters wis in 'e passage aside 'e glory-hole door, though of coorse ye daardna turn't on in the summer. It wis bad enyeuch in 'e winter files makin' sure 'e heat wis on. Niver min' 'at, though, it's nae winter I'm spikkin aboot.

Eence 'e warmer days cam — 'is wis last 'ear — an' ye could keep 'e back door open, I noticet a lot o' little beasties comin' in. Fin 'e licht geed on at nicht, 'ey'd bizz aboot it. Haad awa fae 'e bluebottles, though, naebody peyed attention till 'em. Noo 'an aan ye'd get a bite 'at raised an' reedened 'e skin, bit 'ere wisna much o' that. It's jist aboot 'e eyn o' 'e simmer 'at ye daarna gang till 'e heid o' 'e gairden for fear o' gettin' bitten. If ye pick a flooer or twa, or hae a hagger at 'e hedge, neesht mornin' yer cweets'll be aa up, gey sair, an' yer wrists, like enyeuch yer back an', warst o' aa, in anaith 'e oxters. Fit ondeemous beasts 'is is ye canna ken 'cos ye canna see 'em, though there m'n be a lot aboot. Onywey, they're amon' 'e girse an' 'e flooers an' 'e leaves o' 'e beech-hedge, an' they bide there as lang as they're nae disturbit. I dinna even like tae cut 'e green at 'at time. Fin I div, nae tae be black-affrontit be 'e length o' the foggage, there's nae question bit fit it'll be intill 'e eyntment tin afore bedtime.

There cam a time fin I noticet 'ere wis an aafa lot o' moths aboot 'e hoose. In 'e extension at 'e back, far 'ey cam in fae ootside, 'ere wis 'e odd mothie, sma' eens wi' licht broon wings. They took a fyow turns aboot 'e place, got a bit o' a scaam on 'e electric licht bulbs, an' syne they jist disappeared. I wisna botheret aboot 'e-em. Bit in 'e wall o' 'e stair, 'ere wis fit lookit like anither breed athegither. Ye'd notice 'em on 'e curtains o' 'e stair-windae, an' on 'e wa', an' on 'e grey-pintit widden uprichts o' 'e bannister, an' some got

intill 'e dinin'-room, an' 'e rooms up 'e stair. I happent tae
mention 'is moths, an' oh, they were jist normal for 'is time
'o 'ear. I didna jist agree, but ye niver won be conterin'; aa 'e
same, a fyow days later 'e plastic baggie wis haaled oot o' 'e
glory hole. 'E plastic wis holet in a curn places, an' 'ere wis
nae doot it hid been a great hame for God kens foo mony
maivs amon' 'e bran, as lang's bran wis. But fit she took oot
wis naething bit sids, as I saa fin I cairried it up till 'e heid o'
'e gairden, an' haavert 'e pyock wi' ma knife tae let 'e birds
an' ony ither hungry craiters get at fit wis left. Ye ken, it lay
for days an' naething touched it. Ye'd a thocht there wis
something queer aboot it. it wis 'e rain an' 'e win' in 'e eyn at
did awa wi't, an' maybe it wis' o' some eese for muck, though
fit wi' 'e big sycamore in ae nyeuk an' a haathorn in 'e idder,
there wisna air an' licht eneuch for much in 'e wye o' vege-
tables, an' fither the kitchie-gairden bit got muckit or no
made little odds.
     Noo, 'is moths fae 'e brodmel in 'e glory hole wis big.
They hid lang kinna bodies, an' a rich, dark broon colour 'at
fairly gart 'em stan' oot on a licht wa. For a start 'ere wisna
aa that mony, an' though I k-nackit 'e odd een or twa on 'e
wye up till 'e bathroom — they ay cam oot fin it wis jist
comin' on tae gloamin' — I thocht little aboot it for a fyle.
     In 'e middle o' 'is, I got a fortnicht tae look aifter 'e place
be masel, a job I ay likit, though I hid tae min' tae keep tee
wi' fool socks an' sarks an' hankies, bit 'at didna hinner lang.
I ay managed tae mak mait tae masel aa richt tee, an' I could
get vrocht awa at ma bitties o' writin' withoot 'e television
dirlin' in ma lug. I aften sat lang intil 'e evenin' wi' 'e back
door open, lettin' e air blaa aboot 'e place, an' listenin' till
'e chirps an' fustles o' the birds as 'ey sattled doon for 'e
nicht. Be 'is time 'e cats 'at stravaigit aboot hid geen inside,
nae forgettin' 'e rent-a-cat 'at aften cam tae sleep in 'e hoose,
an' syne held on its roons. Gweed kens far it cam fae, bit it
wis weel fed, an' a freen'ly breet, an' it wis ay a bit o' company if ye no't that. It's a fine kinna time, 'e gloamin'.
     Ay fin I geed up 'e stair 'ere wis mair moths. I began tae
keep 'e kitchie door shut tae haad 'em oot o' 'e sittin' room.
Fin I pit on 'e passage licht, I'd look aroon an' spot 'e broon
shapies. At first it wisna sae hard tae connach 'em wi' the
pint o' ma finger, an' fin I'd cleared the stair as far as I c'd
judge, I'd hae a scan roon 'e spare room an' ma ain bedroom.
Half-a-dizzen wis a low coont, an' even though the baggie 'at
bred and maitit 'em wis gone, they seemed tae hae an aafa

pooer o' appearin'. Fit wis mair, ye'd a thocht they kent 'ere
wis something gettin' at 'em, for aifter a fyow nichts they
didna bide still in 'e wye o' moths, bit gin ye made a move
they'd be up an' awa. A lot o' 'em got in till 'e heich bit o' 'e
ceilin', oot o' ma reach. I took an aal' paper, faalt it intill a
cudgel an' let lick at 'em wi' 'at. Still there wis mair farrer up,
an' I'd tae start haivin' 'e paper abeen ma heid fae a step on 'e
stair tee till 'e riggin, an' files I got een an' files I didna. I'd
finish up pechin', an' aifter half-a-dizzen close misses ye'd
fairly get yer dander up an' start at 'em withoot takin' richt
time tae aim, an' at's nae ma usual wye o' workin'. Anither
queer thing: ony ye knockit aff 'eir perch wi' 'e win' o' 'e
paper wid wheel, wheel aboot yer heid, till ye begood tae be
confoondit, an' ye'd start haadin' yer breath for fear o'
sookin' een in. It didna maitter foo hard ye tried tae keep yer
e'e on 'em tae see far they'd licht, 'ey meeved 'at quick an'
quairt ye'd seen loase 'em.

'Is geed on for a lot o' nichts. Fin ye wis oot o' 'e hoose be
day ye'd think o' 'em in 'e stair-wall, an' tryin' tae settle 'e
question, I bocht some packets o' Mothaks an' sprayed 'em
aboot 'e hoose, hingin' 'em up amon' claes, drappin' 'em in
ahin byeuks, layin' 'em on shelves an' peltin' a hanfae intae
the glory hole itself till ye'd 'a thocht aa livin' beas' wid 'a
smoored. Did it mak a difference? Did it hell. The moths
dreeve on as afore, an' I doot they startit tae spread mair
aboot 'e hoose, for I got a fyow in 'e dinin'-room.

Aifter a file I wis thinkin' aboot 'em near aa 'e time. I
geed roon ilky room mair'n twice a nicht, feelin' ay mair like
'e Kommandant o' 'e prison-camp at Belsen as I poppit een,
syne anither against 'e wa'. I wid dream aboot 'em. The first
thing I did in 'e mornin' wis tae see if I could spy oot ony o'
'e buggers, afore I scrapit ma phisog an' geed masel a gweed
dicht doon wi' saip an' watter as I ay dee. I'd shak ma claes
tae see if ony moths fell oot o' 'em. I'd heist 'e valance o' 'e
bed — weel, it wisna a valance exactly, jist a cover 'at hung
doon a' roon — tae see there wis neen there. At ma wirk in 'e
office, or at meetin's, nae maitter foo I wis catchet up in
maitters o' ootstandin' importance (for 'e meenitie, onywey),
ony dark spot aboot 'e place wid draa ma e'en an' 'e thocht
o' moths wid flit throwe ma heid like 'e eident stabbin' o' a
coorse conscience. An' hame I'd gang an' intae 'e slachter
again.

I widda shut ma bedroom door, bit a wa'-tae-wa' carpet
hid been laid, an' ye'd a deen damage tryin' tae reemish 'e

door tee, an' mair haalin't open again, so I jist left it open a
crackie. It's fine tae streek yersel oot on yer bed if ye've been
scoorin' on aa day, an' 'is nicht I wis glaid tae lie doon an'
steek ma e'en, though nae withoot a hinmist look aroon
for ony o' 'at naisty broon craiters. Nae sign o' onything.
Aa richt, let 'e inhibitions o' 'e day slip, forget aboot 'is
'ferocious work ethic' 'at Northeast bodies is blamet for
haein', even if 'ey wirk in 'e sooth, stop thinkin', dream a
bittie aboot yer freen's, an' aff ye go tae sleep.

Aye, I did. Bit I wisna athegither easy. There wis a droll
kinna feelin' in 'e air, an' though I'd seen nae moths they
werena aa 'at far oot o' ma thochts. Ye ken 'at queer 'eemir a
body gets intill files, fin 'e kinna slips oot o' 'e clay mool', an'
floats aboot lookin' doon at 'imsel', hooseless in a wye, bit
tied tae the bleed an' muscle an' been tee? Weel, 'at wis
'e wye o't 'at nicht. I c'd see 'e room fine, an' 'e bed, an' me
on't. An' throwe 'e crack in 'e door cam a fyow broon bodies,
they begood tae swarm like bees, ay mair comin' in, an' niver
a soon' fae ony o' 'em, keepin' in a ticht, roon' ba', maybe
nae aa 'at ticht for ye c'd see throwe't, bit still it wis a gey
solid like collection.

I'm een o' 'is fowk 'at likes tae start sleepin' flat on their
stamach, ae airm stracht doon, 'e ither at an angle, an' ma
nieve half steekit aside ma chin. Though I start 'at wye, I've
aye noticet 'at be mornin', I'm ower clean 'e conter road, flat
on ma back, wi' ma han's up tae ma kist like a corp waiting
fir 'e trump tae soon'. As lang's I wis on ma face, the moths
jist hoveret, 'e hale birn swayin' back an' fore a bit, bit 'ere
wisna a lot o' meevement, at least neen ye could jist see,
though their wings ma'n 'a' been wafflin up an' doon jist
eneuch tae haad 'em floatin'. I meeved fae 'e richt tae 'e left
side, swappin airms, bit 'e pilla wis a bittie heich or aan 'e
cover wis lirkit, I dinna ken fit, it wisna richt comfortable,
sae I furled roon wi' ma face oot abeen 'e blankets, took a
deep breath or twa, syne sattled doon again.

Noo 'e swarm cam tae life. It drifted ower jist abeen ma
face. For aa 'at ye'd ken, it startit tae split up, till ye c'd see
twa sma' pucklies an' a big een. They come hoverin' ower's
an' as I breathed oot they raise a bittie, an' as I breathed in
they cam a bittie closer, like a balloon balanced on 'e tap o'
an updracht. 'Is geed on for a wee fylie. Syne, in 'is aafa
quairtness, ma mou' opent a bit as a sleepin' man's mou' dis.
Wi' 'at, 'e moths meeved. The twa sma' pucklies geed for ma
nose, an' the bigger een for ma mou', a kinna cheenge o' a

glory hole. Some stray eens geed on fleein', back an' fore. I
shut ma mou', bit 'e moths were in. I sookit air throwe ma
nose, bit hit wis blockit, an' drawin' in blockit it mair. I tried
tae hoast, bit ma throat wis steekit an' fecht as I likit nae
breath c'd I get. In a meenit or twa ma nieves lowsent. Ma
een hid niver opent an' they niver wid. The fyow moths
left hoveret a meenitie mair, syne vanished fae sicht. Fae the
bed, there wis nae movement. Fae the left-han' wick o' ma
mou' cam a thin trail o' broon stuff, like 'e slivers at ran doon
'e chin o' aal Hatton at hame, fin 'e cam tae help ma fadder
tae brak muck, aye cha-chaain' at 'eez tebacca, an' 'ere wis a
sprinklin' o' darker specks tee.

Fin I wakent 'e neesht mornin', there wis a weet spot
aside ma heid on 'e pilla. Bit there wis nae sign o' moths
aifter 'at, it wis jist a clean toon. A lot 'o months later, I wis
kirnin amon' cardboord boxes an' books in een o' 'e rooms,
knockin' aff stew, an giein some files o' paperies a dunt on 'e
fleer. Fit fell oot o' een bit a moth-grub, fite wi' a black neb,
an' 'e biggest I've ivver seen. 'Ere's an aafa books an' papers
aboot 'e hoose. An' aa this wa'-tae-wa' carpets, ye canna see
fit's in anaith. An' 'e glory hole's as fu' as ivver it wis, an' 'e
smell o' Mothaks his worn aff. I'm nae lookin forrit tae
simmer.

Raymond Friel

SCENES FROM CHILDHOOD

in memoriam Mary Alice Friel, 1900-1989

And the end of all our exploring
Will be to arrive where we started
And know the place for the first time.
                    T.S. Eliot, 'Little Gidding'

1

A second cousin from the States
had them all off pat — the Willie's,
the Danny's, the Con's, the Gerald's,
all the clay-pipe-smoking Irish.
We found her coffee, and listened.
I thought she was someone famous
(her perfume filled the sitting-room).
And then she *had* to have photos.
So down we went to the back-green
and under a darkening sky
the four of us posed patiently,
smiling weakly into someone's past.

2

On a hot summer afternoon
we sat, in shorts, on the pavement,
our palms to the warm grimy slab,
backs to the wall, faces held up
to the sun. Then Coffey rifted.
Sun-bathing was not on. Pleasures
had to be all the time and quick.
With a yell we were off running —
to rocks, to old trees, to water.
But nothing could replace that warmth.
In dreams I lay on the warm slab —
borne, protected, absolutely still.

3

I stood at the top of the slope,
the rope, now still, in front of me,
all the rest waiting, looking up.
I was sure they could hear my heart
and see how much I was trembling.
But wanting so much to be part
I would go. I had to, had to ...
clenched, I flung myself towards it,
out through the whistling air, caught
and swung, holding on for dear life.
There the world emptied of terror,
the whole thing relaxing to my swing.

4

My first visit since being born.
My first real smell of hospital.
It was horrible. I stayed close
as we echoed the corridors.
'Where's Granda? Mu-um!' 'Ssh! In here.'
I didn't see my grandfather
but a figure wrapped in plastic
which moved in slow recognition.
He reached and found a packet of
hard mints, but couldn't break them.
The yard's joiner couldn't break them.
And I did, giving half to Martin.

5

Before the hard knock on the door
I knew. Awake, I heard the steps,
tired scrapes after six flights of stairs.
It was uncle Hugh, his deep voice
sounding strange in the house, the rooms
more used to our, much lighter sounds.
I knew the reason he had come.
I knew the room door would open
and Mum come over to me first.
I sat up in bed to listen,
to hear my first bad news in life --
I could not believe the sound was mine.

6

Loitering back one day from school,
someone told me he was home.
And I took off like a mad thing
as if it was only my legs
that knew how much he meant. I tripped
and crashed headlong on the pavement.
Cut, bruised and breathless, I got home.
There he was, all four years of him.
But different. 'Hiyah, buddy,'
he said. It made me uneasy.
For he was much cockier now.
He had been touched by the strange outside.

7

Seeing the heavy-booted men
evacuate to the siren.
Some running, all walking quickly,
pouring out the massive entrance.
Now there is a different view.
With most of the buildings away
there is vaster light and more hills.
The faceless clock-tower is last,
like a lost and wandered old man,
dying just to be done with it.
Only this time the drop is there,
the good son never having made it.

8

And Mum in the small scullery,
busy to an old swing number,
singing, left alone to her thoughts
and me somewhere about, restless —
waiting for the age of reason,
saying the little I could say,
fidgety while time took its time.
But then it was the seventies —
exhausted after the sixties
and whatever it was happened
and before the nineteeneighties
and the simplest credo of all.

9

Mum bent over to do my tie.
A quick brush — shoulders, lapels, back.
She kissed me off on my way,
guarded by the glow of habit.
We conspired as long as we could
behind lifted desk-tops, until
Miss Farquharson began the class.
Poems, we were told, had to rhyme,
like hymns at mass or limericks.
I was to write on astronauts —
I couldn't get a rhyme for sky,
couldn't get a damned rhyme at all.

10

The hurricane was a classic —
a bush rolled across the dark street;
the gale swept up to the window,
rapping, howling. Lightning appeared,
in silence, like a shroud. Thunder —
the worst sound I had ever heard.
My skin tightened into goosebumps.
I looked up at the Sacred Heart.
The taut face softened into speech ...
havering, the lips much too fast;
light oozing from the open chest,
the eyes fixed in the stare of poor art.

11

I rehearsed my one line again.
Said evenly, like a spondee —
two syllables of a language
none of us will ever master
(although many can pass themselves).
The ciborium floated near.
The cold plate touched under my chin.
Knuckles close. Whiteness entered in.
In my new mind reason began.
My first thought gathered, uncertain
of its sounds, its meaning —
God rested on my tongue. Grace danced.

12

My grandmother came from Rathlin,
off the northern coast, as a girl.
She was born with the century,
her age rhyming with great events,
neither too much concerning her.
My grandfather sits in a lull,
dissipated, out of temper.
She barges the door, carefully,
holding out two steaming platefuls,
her eyes on the table. Clacking
china, we miss the silence —
the ghosts, the shouting about money.

13

The tenement bled its people,
losing whole families at a time.
Drawn, not by condemnation
but change as seen by the Town Hall.
There was no talk of ways of life
or passing. Just boxes and hassle;
shouting carrying up the close;
grunts as unwilling furniture
was inched, bumped, down the narrow stairs
and humped into the waiting vans.
So we left. The place heard echoes,
hearing the taps of demolition.

14

I do not know where it came from,
whether from within or without,
only that one day it was there
and I was touched by the future.
The best dressed I had ever been
I sat waiting to be summoned,
my answer getting worse and worse.
'Raymond Friel.' The door was opened.
The Bishop smiled at his large desk.
His voice was rich and magical.
I don't know what my answer was
but it was over — I was out
breathing deeply of the blessèd air.

15

Heading fast for the next eight years,
I got stuck on eternity,
got sold on generosity.
I learned what to do with secrets,
eagerly telling no-one else.
We all drove up to see me off.
Driveway gates closed on a childhood.
In the rush into the priest's arms
I didn't look round, didn't see
Mum lingering back, wondering,
knowing intuitively then
what I would take years to half-perceive.

16

She sat by the open window,
staring out over the river.
'Is anybody home?' She smiled
and disappeared in. A big hug.
I sat, with tea, by the fireplace.
The silence was warm, was welcome.
I looked through into the kitchen
and out the back, to the long grass
where the boy used to hide himself,
and the boy still does. It struck one.
' 'Yi still writing those poems, son?'
Her voice, her face, reality.

Robin Fulton

A FALSE DREAM

The church was grey, squat, low beneath tall sycamores.
No chance for ivy.
I watched it for decades, heard the rooks and the bell.
What could he mean, then,
pointing across the strath, 'You'll remember the church?'
'*That* was never there!'
He smiles, as if I've been away too long to know.
A glimpse of crumbling
ochre, like high walls I once saw in Avignon,
but mostly a green
windowless impenetrable cliff-face — ivy
now holds up the stone.

He makes a large gesture — he who hated 'largeness' —
and boasts: 'That's like me,
all empty now, nothing left to feel the lack of,
nothing left to mourn!'
What do I say to father who is not father?
'You're a short-circuit
in my brain, the right face, the right voice, the wrong style.
Not your style. Not *you*!'
In true dreams the dead are always in character.
This false dream, I pray,
will not persist, like a bad note on a record,
coming round with the years, coming round with the years.

THE GREEN BOAT, THE NIGHT WIND AND THE BIRCH

An inner harbour. Black, still, deep.
A long way
round I have to go, the more
time I take the more I need
to reach you — why are you aboard
an old green
fishing-boat, as if we had
urgent reasons to be gone?
You haven't noticed how the boat
has edged out
leaving silent fatal inches
I can't jump or swim, between.

A world I am about to lose
when dry night
wind cascades like rivers on
moonlit roofs. It says 'You're *here*.'

The birch behind the house has lost
its last leaf.
Something else I could have watched.
Something else the dead won't see.

Janice Galloway

PLASTERING THE CRACKS

It was more serious than I at first supposed. Not that I hadnt
known the place needed attention. I knew all right: there was
a lot to do and I was quite confident I would manage. For
the most part, I was right. But when I started in that back
room, peeling back that first strip of bedroom paper, the
issues became more complex. Plaster clung and came away
with the paper, leaving soft craters in the wall, pouring little
rivers of silt when I touched them. It was regrettable but
obvious I would need help. I tore down the rest of the paper
anyway, letting more plaster drop and lie among the castoff
bits. If I had to hire someone, the room was going to look its
worst. I wanted my moneys worth.

I researched the HOME HANDYMAN ENCYCLOPEDIA
that night. There wasnt much in the way of advice but I
managed to find some information about structural damage
and that made me feel a bit better. I could drop in some background knowledge, sound knowledgeable so they wouldnt
try any fast-talking or bumping up the cost. The services
page in the local paper had plenty of small ads, all different.
I scanned each in turn and chose two plain minimalist efforts,
ringing them heavily with black biro.

The callbox at the end of the street was working and I
got through first try. Arrangements were polite and brief:
both could come round to estimate next morning within half
an hour of each other. The whole business had taken less
than five minutes to set up — smooth as silk. I made a few
calculations in my head on the way back: a couple of days
for the plastering, maybe another fortnight for my work on
the rest of the house, then move the furniture in. It could be
done no bother. I pencilled the notes into my jotter when
I got in and poured myself a whisky. I read the HOME
HANDYMAN till it was too dark.

Next morning, I didnt need the alarm. I was up and
shopping for warm rolls and a morning paper before seven.
Two jumps ahead. The first man was at the door by eight.

He was thin and dark, belonging to the more detailed of the two ads. His inspection of the room unaided took six minutes. He was chatty but pretty po-faced. I had to understand it was more than just plastering the cracks. The whole room would need to be stripped down and resurfaced, some floor panels replaced and the old fireplace could be knocked away. Did I know there was rising damp too. He could do the lot for a fixed price of £200 and begin in a fortnight. When I didn't say anything he told me to think it over. Phone in a few days, check the estimate; let him know. He let himself out.

The next one came twenty minutes later. He had a red face, not much breath and an overtight shirt. His trousers sagged. A woollen bunnet jammed too far down his brow made it hard to see his eyes and I lost concentration on what he was saying till I realised he had stopped. Then I took him through. He went in gingerly, padding at the walls. I was going to leave him to it, then something hooted behind me and I wheeled back. He was facing me directly, too close. The face under the bunnet was rawer in the pale light, his clothes dustier. Another hoot and a rumble, then the fists gesturing near my face. He was explaining something but I couldnt catch it. Just couldnt get the drift at all. It was as though he had a terrible speech defect and no teeth. He kept going though, repeating the same things a few times and miming with his hands. I got the gist it was an estimate. I repeated it: he could do the plasterwork and brick the fireplace for £50. That wasnt it. I had got it wrong: he held up three fingers, sighed and wrote in pencil on the wall. £30. He could do the work for **£30** and start as soon as I liked. I asked him to start next morning, and a smile spread under the hat as I shook his hand, a huge hand with hair all the way down to the nail. My own disappeared inside it. I went with him to the back door and gave him a key in case I was out when he arrived, then waited, waving, till he was out of sight round the corner. That was it. I was pleased with the morning's business. I had thought of everything, hired someone to work for me at knock-down rates: I could handle things. I was nobody's fool. Nobody's mug.

Some time after 11.30 next morning, he arrived. I heard the word LATE as I let him in, but couldnt recall having specified a time and said nothing. In any case, he had already begun shuttling between a blue van outside and the bedroom filling the place with stuff; floury sacks, plastic bins, canvas bags, big polythene pokes full of grey powder; tins of putties, cans, small foil-covered squares and fattily transparent paper bags. I watched from the corner of an eye. On the fourth or fifth journey, he went into the room and reappeared simult- aneously at the back door. The second self had the sun be- hind it, and was smaller and thinner. When it came down the lobby it was another man altogether. I was a bit shaken any- way, and went back to fitting the carpet. It wasnt long till I started enjoying myself. I liked cutting the hemp, the awk- wardnesses and angles of the room. I had a new ruler. As I worked, soft shuffles on the other side of the wall increased my concentration. Grating whispers. Stone, sand, knuckles on board: a cushion of low, male voices. There were two of them now, bridging the space between our separate rooms with muffled somethings. Wool and foam parting roughly under the stanley knife, human warmth seeping beneath the skirting.

Shortly after one, I went out for a hot pie and a dough- nut from the bakery. The cooker wasnt fitted in yet and besides, I liked going there for the savoury scent of it and the heat. I was going to spoil myself since Id finished the carpet. An overturned cardboard box did for a table and the bakery pokes for plates. Even so, the feel of the place still wasnt right. I could hear myself too plainly, moving about, and realised what I was missing was the company. I got out the radio and turned on whatever there was to fill the space. I started to wonder if they were eating, too. Maybe they were eating just as I was, hearing my radio. Maybe they liked the sound of me through the wall as much as I had enjoyed them.

Now there was nothing at all. The last part of the grey meat went cold in my fingers as I listened for them listening. When I noticed, I threw it in with the carpet offcuts and slithered the grease off down the sides of my jeans: Id have a bath later. I could induce no interest in the doughnut and put it back inside the poke: it would keep. I turned the radio down and slid a fresh blade into the yellow stanley knife.

KETL

A word and a sound like a tearing sheet made me turn abruptly.

KETLHEN IH

The fat man crammed the livingroom doorway. I had heard nothing of his approach and here he was right inside the room, speaking. He sipped self-consciously from an in- visible cup to help me with the words.

KETTLE. ONY TEA.

I got up and backed him down the lobby, gesticulating into the space behind him as I walked forward. Once we got to the kitchen, I pointed out the kettle and ran the cold water too hard to demonstrate his welcome to it. The wool bobble nodded. Mushrooms of hairy flesh popped between his shirt buttons as he moved. Under a thick lip of fat, settled on the waistband, his trouser catch was open. I flicked my gaze away quickly but he was happy at the taps and hadnt seen me looking so I slipped back out. Back down the tunnel of the hallway, into the brightness behind the livingroom door. Snug crush of nylon pile under my knees. I was absorbed for the rest of the afternoon, wiring.

At 4.30, a muffled shout hurled up the lobby and the bobble hat pushed round the door.

SUZ SUZ THIDAY

He filled his lungs heavily several times while I said nothing.

BACK THIMORRA OKAY

SOAKAY HEN

he insisted as I tried to get up, a goodnatured dismissal as he saw himself out. Irritation at my own cluelessness hung on through the diminishing sound of feet. I hadnt been able to hear him right. No, *that wasnt it.* I had heard perfectly well. It was more that I didnt seem able to get to the bottom of what he was saying. I couldnt work out a meaning. It reminded me of a habit I got into as a child, something that passed the time on long bus journeys. I would let the engine noise sink me into a kind of hypnosis till the sound lost its significance. Then when people spoke, their words became simply noise, disembodied from sense. Conversation became at once incomprehensible and foreign, a soothing, threatless music to block out exteriors. I could switch it on at will. I encouraged it. But when it began to affect me unbidden I was frightened and stopped the practice by sheer effort of will. Now, a shadow of that fear crept into the bare livingroom and up my neck, till a sudden raucous farting from the street chased me to the window. An ancient exhaust on the carcass of a blue van. I clutched the sill and watched it pass; T G BOYD BUILDER and a snatch of bobble hat.

I was painting when they let themselves in, calling their arrival down the hall. The fat man flooded the doorframe. MAKE TEA FIRST EH. It was quite clear, I heard him fine. There was also a promise of self-containment about it that let me off having to make silly smalltalk. Gratefully, I shouted through for him to take some rolls if he liked, and soon after, heard them in gentle, manly rifts of appreciation through our wall. I thought of them in there, in my bedroom, eating buttered gifts with hot tea.

By lunchtime I had the makings of a headache. The narrow windowframe needed a great deal of concentration and I had already smeared the glass twice. Maybe I needed my dinner. It would be nice to be out for a wee bit of fresh air too, away from the paint fumes. Only a short walk to the bakery, but it would do.

I selected a sausage roll and an empire biscuit. The woman touched my hand giving me change and called me dear. I was feeling better already. The lobby was thick with dust when I got back; enough to make the air visible. Dull thuds from the bedroom confirmed they had started on the heavier stuff, knocking away the brickwork or something. While I made my tea, the thumping got worse. There was no milk. I looked around a bit before realising it was likely in with them — in the bedroom with their morning tea things, but I wasnt going to interrupt their concentration or my privacy to collect it; it wasnt that important. I settled for black and walked back through chalky clouds, roaring like dry ice under the door.

I enjoyed the food. Im sure I did. After all, I had been painting all morning and I was hungry. But I was increasingly more aware of the headache all the time I was eating. I thought it was most likely the noise from the back room that was doing it, or the hangover of turps. I rubbed my temples as another crash like rockfall billowed the wall, followed by muttering and laughter: I clearly heard the word STARVIN and others less distinct. I picked up my brush when it stopped.

It was a long afternoon. The window smudged to spite me and I got fed-up wanting it done nicely in favour of merely getting the thing finished. My eyes frazzled as the paint wiggled off the brush end like white insects. I was still at it when I heard them packing up to leave.

That time already. I took their tip, waited till they had gone for sure then wandered up the lobby. Some tea, maybe, and yesterday's doughnut to keep me ticking over. A wee doughnut would do me fine.

It wasnt there. I checked all the likely places and a few of the more bizarre. I knew I hadnt thrown it out and I knew I hadnt eaten it either. I caught a glimpse of the bag near the sink. Its whiteness hurt as I picked it up and I had to peer to make out some thin pencil scrawl written on the lower edge. It was a message. THANKS FOR THE DOGNUT. TG's writing. He must have assumed it had been part of a lot with the rolls. Then I remembered about the milk it would still be through there as well. Right. I would collect it now. It was time I checked up on what they had been doing in there anyway. It had been two days after all, and it couldnt be far from finished. Hadnt even expected them to stay this long, not for £30. Not for £30 for two of them. Christ. I could hear my head fizzing like Alka-Seltzer. What if the estimate had been partial or something? for materials only, and labour was extra? What if I hadnt understood? I rushed down the lobby, then pulled up stiffly at the closed face of the bedroom door. I took two deep breaths. Then I twisted the handle and walked unflinchingly inside.

Inside.

It was light and dark at the same time and the walls were moving. They were sliding and changing colour in huge suppurating spots. In the middle of the textured ceiling there was a glittering ball of mirror chips, rotating and sparking out light that turned on the wall in formless, spreading blobs. For a while, I was too taken in with this to see much else. It was only with much effort I managed some furtives glimpses of the rest of the room. There were long poles in one dim corner, leaning like clothes props, and toolsacks, pregnant with hidden lumps. Bottles of dark fluids, metal bars, cups of powder. Near the blinded window, a huge sofa, piles of magazines, empty cans. And the remains of my doughnut. Around and under everything, the floorboards were still bare, the walls were still meshed with soft cracks. I couldnt see what they had been doing to the fireplace since it was masked with an old-fashioned firescreen, heavily embroidered with leering birds of paradise and peacocks whose eyes glowed and receded in the coloured rays from the ceiling.

And there was the milk, inches away, near my foot.

Seeing it there restored some of my equilibrium. Just a green and white carton with dark brown lettering and a cartoon drawing of a cow relaxing on a milkstool. I fixed my eye on the smile of the cow, trusting it to keep the rest at bay. For the rest — I knew even as I was watching — the rest was not really there. It was ridiculous. If I ignored it, it would go away. My head pounded as I stopped to pick up the carton and walked backwards out of the room, keeping my breath steady till I got out. Then I pulled the door shut too hard and

loosened more plaster. I could hear it scratching against the
boards inside. Too bad. I had to stop it spreading to the rest
of the house, keep it under control. Then I knew that was
daft. My own over-active imagination. I wanted to smile. HA
HA I laughed up the hall; HA HA along the tunnel into the
dark. Time I had that tea and a bit of a rest. Yes, a nice cup
of tea then I would relax for the night. My mind was made
up to forget the whole thing till the next morning. Yet I tip-
toed to the bathroom and moved the sleeping bag round on
the floor before I went to sleep. Better safe.

Accordion music. Accordion music woke me. I sat up
still inside the sleeping bag to listen. There was a rhythmic
swishing noise as well, and both were coming from very near.
They were coming from the bedroom. I heard a clear single
word: HOOCH — and some undistinguished guffawing. I
checked the alarm. It was well after 10. I had overslept and
they had let themselves in, had started work in the back
room. Then I wondered if they had come up the lobby as
usual, opened my door, looked in on me when I was asleep.
Maybe spoken about me, laughed about me when I couldnt
hear. I was irritated, embarrassed and confused. I didnt want
to go to the bathroom if they were in the hall either. The
easy way out would be to go across the road — wash and
breakfast in the bakery coffee bar and give myself time to
come to. I would think of something then. Laughter welled
up behind me as I slammed the front door.

It worked, though. By the time I returned I felt much
brighter. I made a lot of noise with the front door so they
would hear. I had worked out a plan as I sat in the shop and
knew exactly what I was doing. It was time I pulled myself
together and started moving around my own home as though
it was my own home. They would walk all over me if I didnt.

I strode purposefully across the carpet and down the
lobby, then stopped at the bedroom door to listen for my
moment. They were talking. The words SOON and OKAY
came through the accordion tunes, then TG's voice cut clear,
making perfect sense NO BE LONG NOO and sighing.

It took the wind out of my sails. If everything was well in
hand, there would be no need to get heavyhanded. They
seemed to be gathering stuff together. I slipped away into the
kitchen. The first thing I saw was the milk carton. A fresh
one. They had bought me a new pint. AYE. NEARLY BY.
DO WIYA BATH EH. I kept the voices in my ears and picked
up the carton, holding it to my chest. Things were all right.

Everything was under control. TG began to sing tunelessly in a light baritone.

I didnt need the tea but I made it anyway and went to sit with it in the livingroom and check my list I had written.

1   SORT OUT BUSINESS — SEE ROOM!
2   HOW MUCH LONGER?
3   Second coat on interior door.

I scored out 1 and 2, ringing 3 with a flourish, then switched on the radio for the shipping forecast. I was almost relaxed.

The door proved easy after yesterday's window frame. Paint rolled off the brush in merging strips while people talked about gardens on the radio. When it got boring, I switched off and went on with the paint. So I didnt notice the silence at first. But it thickened as time passed and I soon checked my watch. After 2. That meant no sound at all from next door for well over three hours. They couldnt have gone already because I hadnt paid anything. And the van was still there on the other side of the road: T G BOYD murky under the filth. I moved quietly to the bedroom door. Nothing. I tapped at the closed panels, listening hard. Then something bubbled suddenly behind me, the plumbing groaned. Instinctively, I propelled myself forward away from the noise and into the room. I should have known.

There was a deck chair in primary stripes right in the centre of the bare boards. Crushed beer-cans, two billiard cues made a pyre in the corner near a crude newsprint pin-up. Another corner glinted with dustless tools, polished chrome and steel. Breathlessly, I scanned for evidence of their labours. The cracks on the wall nearest me had peeling oblongs of sellotape over their mouths: those higher up seemed completely untouched. An old piece of skirting had been reattached with orange plasticine, bulges of it oozing between the wood and the wall. Some stone had been chipped off the fireplace and lay in a heap where the surround had been. The grate was full of crumpled bits of the DAILY RECORD, strapped in place by a mesh of masking tape. The bubbling noise rose up again, more identifiable this time. The rush and whinny of water. It was coming from the bathroom. Splashing and muted giggling. TG's unmistakable enunciation: SOAP. Then I saw: pencilled on the grubby plaster round the lightswitch, a scribble of noughts and crosses and some words. APRIL FOOL. Water rushed in the bathroom. The bastards were having a bath.

Furious, I lunged for the livingroom and hunted out some paper. I forked the pen out from under the toolbox then sat to write.

OUR CONTRACT IS TERMINATED FORTHWITH. PLEASE COLLECT YOUR STUFF AND LEAVE.

Then I fished out the three £10 notes I had kept in my purse from their first day, waiting for them. Too bad if I had got it wrong: it was all they were getting. I put them with the letter into a manila envelope, sealed it, stormed down the hall and unhesitatingly stuffed the lot under the bathroom door. The sound of towelling stopped abruptly. There was a dry click of paper as a fat hand found the envelope. That was enough. Blazing with trepidation and triumph, I left the house and walked as fast as I could to the bus stop.

All the streetlights were burning when I got back. The van was gone: I had seen that much as I walked up the street. I called out at the back door to make sure: COOEE. But nothing answered. The kitchen was very dark inside, darker even than the road, but I waited till I got used to it and found I could see pretty well without putting the light on. I preferred it that way. I would have a wee look in then plan for tomorrow; check out what had to be done in there and work out how to do it myself. Fresh start. I had my HOME HANDYMAN, my notebook. I would manage.

The doors gaped in a Russian doll series behind me as I made my way through to the bedroom. It was open, and for once the blind was up. I looked. The walls were smooth, the fireplace bricked and flat. The drying plaster had been sanded and a heap of plaster dust smoked in the corner near my kitchen brush. On the white windowsill, outlined in the moonlight, were some bits of paper and something silver. The spare key, a dull, crushed oncer and a note from TG.

CHANGE.

Michael Gardiner

SHIELDS ROAD

I

Are you indoors or out? Are you sure?
Two flights down, the hall with the clean tiled floor,
Calm and warm enough, bar five-minute gales,
Flushes empty at obscure hours, leaving you alone
Slouched below framed pictures, awaiting guests.

But the puzzle can be solved. Take off your coat. Stretch
    your legs,
This in-house shuttle's an apartment in itself —
A front room done up before a grandparent died,
Before these others arrived and sacked it as theirs,
Dressed for outside, and after three or four halts,
Re- re- re- replacing themselves.

The works are locked back — London hasn't swallowed us.
These cars are like pistons flush with casing,
Not rolling-stock rattling along iron tracks.
Pot-rim insects, tugged by eddies,
Electric-shocked and sucked through stone, to the next cave.
Not Newcastle, even. Glasgow's disposition
Is drilled through pavements and indents the very earth,
Sunk forty feet deep into cosmopolitan life.

It's quiet still when one or two dockers at Govan
Trudge in with the final Evening Times,
As if the Clyde were young, and this a 14 bus —
On a dead-beat pilgrimage through West-end sunset;
Not embarrassing the subculture (that's the generic word)
Of Hillhead students who pack the car, fill it with talk,
The maths exam, the Floyd LP, the easy lay.
And the Glasgow drunk, who's part of the act (to show the
    audience
What they're missing), enduring more dizzy circuits, trying to
    get
To a station demolished on modernisation.

Trust these modern-day beaus to snicker, hung-up on realism,
Deliberately sideburned. Their girls in on-purpose My Little
    Ponytails
Half-dream and half-sneer, half-a-little-mixed-up
(But so's half the city).

Funnily enough
When the subway rediscovers a more sinister use,
When the concepts 'out' and 'in' are yanked inside-out,
And the idea's pricked, letting draught air rush away,
The youth will waste first, without make-up or haircare.
We're a motorway from Blighty, and further from the 50s, but
Dungeoned we'll anachronistically chant
Warsongs for spirit, and tunnel in requisitions
Of kerosene lamps, Bovril, horse-blankets.

Despite the commotion upstairs
The station's just the same below, somehow homely.
You see, all it took was some rubble at the entry
To be roomified. But it's darker, it's choked.
A car's stuck half-way to West Street. Remember this city,
With its only plug whipped out the wall and smashed,
With these blocked-up capillaries knotted round its beatless
    heart.
So this must be the living-room.

UNCLE, DYING

In the morning he lay resting. At night he still lay.
After his snooze, not much happened. He weakened, of
    course,
Paled and stopped respiring. He was found limp-necked and
    grey,
Come through from the scullery. It appeared no great force
Had heaved his being to any higher sphere,
He just lay and passed on. We were relieved to see him still,
Not wandering, slippered. My cousin pulled the sheet up, left
    him there.
It seemed strange he couldn't move, couldn't waken up. His
    skin
Once coloured by mates' fists, had fallen to a shade
So sad in him. He cloyed us sometimes — that look,
That eager surprise. A lover, now treated by lemonade,
A sailor's foul mouth come to dribbling mushroom soup.
He looked happy enough. He'd watched racing all day,
But no-one could check bookies' lines any more.
In the morning he lay resting. At night he still lay.
Before supper someone must have left, but I'd have heard
    them slam the door.

William Gilfedder

CHURCH UNITY GLASGOW STYLE

The great ecumenical disaster of our time
Christian unity with a mohican haircut
And skinhead profile
Get the advocates of unitarianism
Batter the general council of world churches
Stamp oot the free thinkers
Mollacate the episcopacy of bishops
Integrate or annihilate
Show charity tae nane
It's either wedlock or the tomahawk
Whit'll it be jimmy.

CITY LIGHTS

Just in case you've ever wondered
Why glow-worm larvae are so thin on the ground
The reason is, the male glow-worm is attracted away
From the small light of the female glow-worm
By the brighter lights of the city
So there.

John Glenday

WAR PICTURES

in memoriam John Goodfellow Glenday

1 Crete 1941

I was Nobody with a rifle
when the paratroopers came.
A Nobody with a rifle
I couldn't fire, guarding
a Nothing I wouldn't remember,
in a Nowhere I'd never forget.

The sergeant sent me up a rotten ladder
to the open, whitewashed roof:
'*Have a quick shufti at what's going on.*'
I crouched by the cistern,
clutching my rifle like
an awkward branch, hoping
to god no one would notice me.

Stukas with folded wings
were falling like gannets
on the road to Maleme.
Then a vague, sporadic gunfire fumbled
closer, smacking grey
cups in the walls below me.

The ladder having been removed
by a panicking lieutenant,
there was nowhere I could run.
So I threw myself upon the blank page
of the roof, praying for all I was,
all I might never be.
My loosened tin hat dotting
the i of me.

2 *Freight*

We spent a week in cattle trucks,
creeping from Greece to the Sudetenland.
The tougher prisoners shoved
their way to the plum spots
by the ventilators, but
the doors stayed locked four days.
We had no choice but to force
our faeces through the nose-high grilles.

Old Harper laughed at that as
he sucked on his empty pipe:
*'Remember son, the strong might
claim the cleaner air,
but they smell of shite.'*

3 *Jockeys Sudetenland 1941*

Jolted awake in
the perpetual twilight
of nowhere, we were moths
pulled to the dusty,
slatted sunlight
and the muffled laughter.

In a meadow by the sidings,
jockeys in their pressed
silks, paraded
in never decreasing
circles.

4   *Dead Meat   Stalag XIIIB*

A double charm
against escape:
Herr Knappek

made us watch
as the camp guards
bayonetted

our tins
of Red Cross
bully beef.

5   *Window*

Long after the contrails
of the bombers had drifted
back to immaculate blue,
tatters of silver paper
tumbled from the sky.

Guards looked at prisoners.
Prisoners looked at guards.
Some blamed it on the Russians.
Others waited for the world to end.

One fellow, knocking
the mud from his boots
against a wall, said
perhaps it was only
God in his little firmament
weeping at the products
of our squandered freedom.

6 Beach Hall, Monifieth. 1946

Doomed by those low,
octobering clouds of June,
another half-cocked venture fails.

But he poses boldly enough
for the camera, thrusting
two ice cream cones no one will buy
at two smiling virgins.
He looks at neither.

Their faces are folded in shadow,
but at the centre of it all
he holds out before him
those two ice creams
like twin lamps of ignorance
and his lame future gleams.

Rod Hart

DREAM TIGER

Waiting, toothless, at the water's edge
for the calm approach of the Indian girl
with the deep brown eyes
and the aching earthenware pot . . .
I lie here nights, dreaming of retirement.
My tongue is in the dust.

'Hello there, Tiger!' Opening an eye
I watch him noise me up.
Coach. Not one of the old school:
no punishing schedule, no punitive regime,
just straight down the line with the protein carrot,
the tempting incentive scheme.

Trust him to saunter in sporting
(Coach is always sporting) that old striped shirt
which makes him look so touchingly like me.
'We're in this together, Tiger,' he remarks,
slapping down a side of beef on the bone.
This cage, this business — this mess?

I flex my stripes, she drops the pot . . .
But I'm no Bengal tiger now, just another
member of the team. Cruel? Coach? No way!
Since the moment I met that inspiring man
he's killed me with kindness
in every way he can.

W.N. Herbert

GREEN DOLPHIN STREET

'Deep in the saul the early scene —
Ah, let him play wi' suns wha can,
The cradle's pented on the een,
The native airt resolves the man!'

'Country in which to reconstruct a self
From local water, timber, light and earth,
  . . .
It matters where you cast your only shadow,'

Scadlippan laneless is
                    meh ainly brose
an aa ma mou cud sup, murgeond up
an murld awa by luv, time-hastenin;
and o ma ithir hert that Eh brak here
thi Ferry's flisks hae cleard ut up at last
Eh hearna meevie nor mavie o'ut:

Here is thi front's charrd auld barbecue
lyk a witch's baby grand,
and here's a crumpilt Courier's flap
lyk a seagull, deean oan thi saund.

Here is Rentokil Hoose's guttirs fu
o pink blossom whaur
meh grandfaithir wiz boarn an photied
wi'iz pipes, afore thon tuneliss war.

And here ur aa thi firemen i thir ingine,
a picter o muneecipal virr:
sittan ootside Vissocchi's
eatan slidirs i thi smirr.

Here is ma Ferry again, inna foarm
that's feery assuts fleet, daurk sails
that sune sall be in nae man's memry,
fleerin'ur leaf-like images up
in ma vishun's fiss, yet ut nivir pales, is
broon assa tinkie at thi berries, nae
Victoriun's pastils lyk a wean's wabbit puke,
nae china cup yi maun
pit thi mulk in furst,
nae bairn left uncurst
by aa'uts scaudin peers,
nae Tonio Kroeger cud mak ut here
whaur thi muse utsel's a scargivnet.

Spence nivir telt thi wey thi sand
sucks thi gless o thi retreatan waatir
intae a sheen lyk suede fae leathir,

an therr's a hinge whaur thi shelf-
slope cheenges til a deepir incline
that's drehd lyk a backbane tae thi beach.

A toothbrush ligs oan uts back
i thi waash o kombu an crisp-packits,
deid-dune fae poalushin thi Castil Rock,

no that uts plaque o plooky weed's awa;
Eh scrambil ower igneous jaas an perch
oot o ma time lyk a seal inna bath.

Nae sugarellie-waatircolors here; aa
metrics dissoalve lyk Embra Rock
an laive yi lukean at Tay's platinum ee

ablow thi suddin-nekkit skeh. Thi renn's
no really left an this blistir o thi meenut's
heat'll hae nae time tae dreh. This ettin's

basin's reddy tae sloosh owre ony
adjective Eh think o an rear back, laivin
'sillery' — Eh'd be a new Tamfule tae nae

be content as sic a trageediun —
but thi best o luck tae Dougliss Dunn.

PICTISH MUSIC PERHAPS

Doon thi frunt Eh pit meh fit oan
ruits that brust thi cauld taur apert
o pehvments, lyk thi last shaukins o
smilodon an mammoth, i thi taury pits

o a buik i ma bairnheid: Eh canna mind
thi pliss. Eh pit meh fingir oan a wurd
i thi dickshunary that precedit whit Eh yaize
an feel ut trummil. Eh canna mind whethir

ut wiz Arbroath or St Andrews and Eh
dinnae ken, but ut wiz inna rowboat, wi
ma grandad, undir thi cleuchs and intae
thi caves, an he pit thon haund Eh scrieve wi

oan ma shoudir an telt me no tae dern
ma een, but opent'iz jaiket an sedd
Eh cud cloich in therr. An sune's thi sun
wiz tint, an aa wiz waatir's saft claps oan

thi boatie's ribs lyk tig, an shillies an
cauts o licht lyk ribbuns in brainches,
Eh hid. An Eh dinna ken whaur Kilchattan
Cave is, save inna buik, but Eh ken o

thi piper that mairchit in, and pleyd,
mairchin in, an thi lugs o thi locals werr
lissnin til thi tintin lilt, a timidinnitus that
peeried an wearied until ut cam

fae titans' cloistirs lyk thi whuspir fae
a bed o oystirs i thi Tay o shells shuttan
lyk applause, feet drappin lyk a tap that
wauks yi, fingirs flappan lyk ribbuns oan

an extractir, drooly slavirs o sand aroond
toyts' jaas haufrisin lyk a cobra-coarnfield til
sum whifflan o thi mune's pu, syne poutir awa
lyk willas oot o thi skail's rouch haund.

Doon thi frunt Eh pit meh fit oan
pasts that buck lyk a whale's split back
an mind o thi gaithrin o thi freens o Poet
MacGonnagal, that near sunk thi Unicorn.

PURITY IN DUNDEE

I was with you all night wherever
you are except the time's different there:

you kiss this thin pane that parts us
wherever we are like scratching the sun.

It lies like a silicone implant fallen from
the sky or a jellyfish on my shoreline

this eye I see you through bone with;
skulls can kiss through thought's maiden-

head which keeps growing back,
stubborn mindless flower of doubt.

To make an image is to lose you,
this presence about my flesh; meanwhile

we are like two watches synchronised,
once again sky strikes a palette from

my head with its white lime and grey
magenta palms, like an ant in

attenuated mittens. It sets us and
parts us and lets us meet endlessly.

ON THE COLD LIDO

Gaubertie-shells at shore
an children lauchin oan
th'esplanade,
a gush-hole atween us,
a ghaist-coal i thi ess o nicht,
a faa o sand tae cairpet.

Th'auld wid steps
i thi middil o thi strand
fur when thi tide is in,
splintirs i ma back:
Eh lukeit doon frae ma starry childhood
oan'ur kaid.

HOUSE OF CLOUDS

These stone palms that press us
together like leaves have sprung

apart to let the bodies follow their
own hours: you are in your busy

past and I slip repeatedly over
the bolt-hole to paradise in Dundee.

I need you to place me in here as
though setting a watch. Other hands

will work us back to this same hour
for the first time. I sit in my grand-

mother's house watching clouds slip
over the rippled glass and aeroplanes

who're looking for their own hour.
Your face defies you by lacking

age, purpose, evangelism; in the act
of love I feel like the horse on which

it becomes clouds, moving silently
beyond all glass, my framing heart.

Richard Jackson

A FUNNY THING

Not far from where I live there's a butcher's shop
Where the assistant looks like Laurence Olivier.
Quite often, if I'm passing, I take a moment off to stop
And watch him over the meat bargains of the day.

It jars at first to find that dignified, expressive face
Whose silent rhetoric can obviate all need to speak
Angled with all its usual precision in such a place;
But follow his hands and you recognise the same technique.

One operates by words, the other, with near-equal skill
    perhaps,
By knife, deftly unseaming carcasses from nave to chaps,
Knowing exactly where and when to apply what force.
Some day I expect to hear him calling for a horse.

Robert Alan Jamieson

A DAY AT THE OFFICE
a drama for three voices

THE OVERSEER
the underling
the timepiece

zero-eight-one-zero
Alarm call
this is what i do
i dream of bees inside the lion
the syrup tin of samson
the riddle me ree
good morning good morning
this is your early morning
is the answer a joke?
this line the punch?
are you awake yet?
it delivers respectful poison
submits its quiet venom
WORK'S EASY RIGOURS ARE YOUR LAST SWEET DREAM
though other music plays at night's death flame
I won't call again
THIS IS YOUR EARLY MORNING
i wake up late
the sleep the answer
the joke on it

zero-eight-two-seven
RUN
huh-huh-puff the cold air
bus
stops
change
upstair
my clinging porridged face clinched grey
the first principle

zero-nine-zero-zero
passing through the door
summoning the lift
the minute hand to
has the second circled
when will it tock?
THE CELEBRATORY INDULGENCE IN EMOTION
ACCOMPANYING RITUAL ACTION
IN THE UNCOLLECTED MIND
IS THE BASIC BUILDING UNIT
IN THE PROCESS OF SOCIAL RENEWAL
caught in the merry dance of being
this same place same time tomorrow

zero-nine-zero-one
the black ink print reads late
A SECOND CHANCE IS NOT AN OPTION
even if i think i m due one
THE PUNCHED CARD SHOWS THE MOMENT'S GONE

zero-nine-three-zero
the firstmost yawn dictates the domino tumble
we tap and push these buttons
SCRIBBLE DOWN IN CARELESS SCRIPT OF SPIDERS
an eyepiece on the yawning city
these figures of the average
FORM WEBS OF PULSED STATISTICS
netting over every target block

zero-nine-four-five
small quantities of lightning
pass through our fingertips
each time we press these keys
this may be the source
of the disorientation in society:
our bodies are largely water
water and electrics do not mix
YOUR EMPTY HEADS PRODUCE A DULLING ECHO
SIMPLE abc's OF TIME
SHOULD BE DISTRIBUTED AMONG YOU

to charge our instinct
we should sleep
while the moon
is waxing strong
to charge our instinct
with the electric off
at the main

one-zero-doublezero
my heart is ticking like a telex
but here in the office
the condition of an organ
is of little concern to the corporate good
which sways upon the shoulder
of the overseer's leer
it sniffs
CURE YOURSELVES AND SO SECURE TOMORROW
in this renewal
you must choose
new versions of your names
and signatures
TRY
a new diet
SPORT
a new haircut
FIND
a new lover
DANCE
at the office party

one-zero-three-zero
in life
as in
coffee breaks
more tales of failure
reach an ashtray grave
than of achievement
we must talk
HIGHER FASTER
deeper closer
never stop this chatter
become the moving dead each night

one-one-three-zero
it's the same old same old
freedom's such a sacrifice
of
say   MONEY   *it*
STATUS
who i am

who am I?
more
than
THIS
neck tie

more wise
than any skin bone sage

THAN ANY OLD FRIEND
CLAIMING YOU'VE BETRAYED SOME TREASURED SECRET

i ll stay a while at this

the pays not bad
an i m so hungry
i
could eat a horse
so long as its meat
and bloody

TOGETHER
WE COULD GO FAR

ME
HERE BEHIND

YOU
IN THERE WORKING

WITH THE SCHEDULE
LAID OUT
ON

MY

MASTER-PLANNER

one-two-one-five
THE BARGAIN'S STRUCK
castaway in sumptuous envy
button-pushing
surmising on
the curious warmth
OF A BLOATED STOMACH
FORGET CONTRACTUAL DIFFICULTIES

feed me
fold me over
lick and stick
me
down

i ll stay
in a specific locality
in your pocket

one-two-five-seven
sneak away to queue
for take-out-eat-away
eatables
what matters it if i am seen
if dignity is tied to conscience
if all is lost at all
the sustenance of bread is no illusion
my jaws apart
i bite
i grind

the hunger stays

ecrof sgnieb elohw a seriuqer ti
to swallow

sometimes i feel about to self combust
the overseer summarises
HE WAS ALWAYS UNRELIABLE
STUCK IN A PERPETUAL RUT
REPEATING SHORT SCANT PHRASES
HARDLY MOVING
NO HOPE OF PROGRESS

but the morsel slides
acids attack
THE SYSTEM WORKS

one-three-three-one

the shuffling train beneath this park
tunnels deeper than i want to go
the thought that i could lose this place
as lightly as i came to live it
leaves me dashing for my desk
my place of doubt
my work

MY OFFICE

securing fingerless deposits
in your numbered credit
hoarding spot

one-four-doublezero
back
belly leaning on the edge
of this cosy three foot precipice
i feel so manifestly safe
IF YOU'LL JUST SIGN HERE
I CAN EXTEND YOUR CONTRACT
THE PENSION SCHEME CAN PROMISE YOU
SOME TRULY RICH REWARDS
FOR LOYALTY YOU'LL GLEAN
ANOTHER SPROUTING SPRING
FRESH APPETITE
GREAT VIGOUR
THE POWER OF SELF-ASSERTION
NO HUMBLE TRADESMAN MOCKS OUR STAFF
RIGHT NOW DISPOSE OF ALL YOUR OLD ADDICTIONS
YOUR FEELINGS OF WORTHLESSNESS
THOSE WORN OUT WORRY BEADS
THE OPPRESSIVE RELIGION
THE LACK OF FAITH
BELIEVE IN THE COMPANY

but please don't fret
if you really want to keep those useless crutches
we can arrange you start
a rehabilitation scheme
the end of which is guaranteed
to make your old bad habits just as sweet and fresh
as when you first so innocently found them
DO YOURSELF A FAVOUR
COME TO THE PARTY

one-four-four-six
THE PRICE IS FIXED ACCORDING TO DEMAND
LET EACH ACCORDING THEIR MEANS DELIVER
i feel no pain, no sense of loss
despite this longing to be free
of certainty

one-five-three-zero
the dark dim has no date in here
begun with capital
we modulate perfection in fluorescent strips
maintain a marathon of concentration
to resist the blanket tricks of time
see each hidden card before its played
and scent the rabbit waiting
up the wizards sleeve
avoiding piles of paper
edging closer to the time where i will meet
and wrestle its accounted tally
THE MASK I WAS ONCE FOLLOWS ME ROUND
THOUGHTS OF OLD FRIENDS, OLD BOOKS
OLD SONGS, OLD FRIENDS
BUD OPEN AT THE SLIGHTEST NUDGE
AND THERE I SULK
BEFORE I SIGNED THE CONTRACT
SAYING PLAINLY WITH MY STANCE
give me your suit
i have ambition
give me your shoes
i ll fill em

A SALARYS NOT HARD TO SPEND
WHEN THERES REPAYMENTS
ON THE MORTGAGE
ON THE CAR LOAN AND THE PLASTIC
WHEN THERES AN EMPTY HOUSE AND LIFE TO PACK

one-six-four-five
youve had long enough to think about it
JUST SIGN HERE AND TAKE THE BOTTOM COPY
you know you really need this, dont you
YOU REALISE THERES NOTHING BUT THIS FOR YOU
same place same time tomorrow
NO FIDDLING DONT BE LATE

one-seven-one-zero
that busker down there in the doorway
makes a better living
and he has no one to demand it
round here
its a cinch knot on a pursers beard
real charity
BUT STILL WE HANG AROUND THE OFFICE
IN PORT IN HOPE
OF WARMING THROATS AROUND THE BIGGEST FIRE
yet
as night sets in
i m standing on the fringe
of every reel
waiting for a walkon part
a certain laugh
to take a taxi home
and not the crowded bus
after a day at the office
i watch from the top deck
as a man from down our street
drops his face on the pavement
while retrieving his hat
HE SHOULD LEAVE WHAT HE CANNOT CARRY
TOO MANY SUPERMARKET BAGS OF UNENDURABLES
WEIGH HIM LIGHT
IN THE SCALE
THAT COUNTS

one-eight-zero-one
in this part of town
a door shuts on
ME
prepare the ground
put down some roots
at dawn for nightfall
a new birth for the self-alone
the tuber sprouts a head
the head opens its eye
sees thinks
its not enough to simply grow
i want to travel
i want to walk
the plant advances
it wants to read the paper wants to watch teevee

one-eight-five-eight
evolving into free time
take plenty of liquid
run in the bath
BUT NAKED AFLOAT THERE
I SEE THEM PEEP
ON TIPTOE
AT MY WINDOW
I DONT MIND
ITS PART OF THE JOB
TO PUT UP WITH THE COMPANY

one-nine-one-one
sit down with hot news dinner
microwoven a la carte delight
tonight
like the ad people eat
count calories in captions
watch the screen version
of the food before
chewing over
the events of a day at the office
a plane has crashed
a politician lied
an actor wrote a book
WHAT ELSE IS NEWS
the headtalkings tie

two-one-five-nine
and i have seen life tonight
have listened to
a hundred plus
opinions
on the many issues
currently in vogue
ALL ROUNDED UP AND RATIONALISED
IT MAKES A TIDY PILE OF PLASTIC
IN THE TV COMPANY FILE
a record of our time
the voice of our time
a sign of our time
the cause of our time
view and counterview
a tale of lust and greed
of passions thrusting hand
and what it grips
LANGUAGE GOUGING MEMORY
MUSIC GAUGING HOPE

two-three-two-one
no such thing as harmless
fantasy
if it was harmless
no one would want it
JUST LEARN TO BE GRATEFUL FOR OFFICIAL RELEASE
switch off the lightning
the moon is

u
p

above the speckled city
a mist descends upon the valley
the crane returns to its rooftop roost
the red car turns
into a bay mare
is parked in the cul-de-sac
s l e e pd r e a m

zero-four-zero-now
d r e a m work
and no will need to do this
the bees are bees
listening for alarm calls
doing with no significance
w o r k e d   o u t
DREAM WORN
THE LION LISTENS
for alarm calls
ENJUNGLED IN THE NIGHT
AWAKENS
in time
ABOVE
the under

David Kinloch

DUSTIE-FUTE

When I opened my window and reached for the yoghurt cool-
ing on the outside ledge, it had gone. All that remained was a
single Scottish word bewildered by the Paris winter frost and
the lights of its riverbank motorways. What can 'dustie-fute'
have to say to a night like this? How can it dangle on its
hyphen down into the rue Geoffroy L'Asnier where Danton
stayed on the eve of revolution? How can it tame this strange-
ness for me or change me into the strange cupolas and flag-
stones I so desire yet still notice everytime I walk on them?
Does the 'auld alliance' of words and things stand a chance
among the traffic and pimps in the Publicis Saint-Germain?
These are the wrong questions. For it's not as if 'dustie-fute'
was my familiar, not as if it could float down like soft gauze
and make the city sneeze so that I could wake up tomorrow
and be able to say bless-you to its snow-covered streets. I
could easily confuse 'dustie-fute' with 'elfmill' which is the
sound made by a worm in the timber of a house, supposed
by the vulgar to be preternatural. This is also called the
'chackie-mill'. These words are as foreign as the city they
have parachuted into, dead words slipping on the sill of a
living metropolis. They are extremes that touch like danger-
ous wires and the only hope for them, for us, is the space
they inhabit, a room Cioran speaks of, veering between
dilettantism and dynamite. Old Scots word, big French city
and, in between, abysmal me: ane merchand or creamer, quha
hes na certain dwelling place, quhair the dust may be dicht
fra his feete or schone. Dustie-fute, a stranger, equivalent to
fairandman at a loss in the empty soul of his ancestors'
beautiful language and in the soulless city of his compeers
who are living the twenty-first century now and scoff at his
medieval wares. And here, precisely here, is their rendez-
vous and triumphantly, stuffed down his sock, an oblique
sense, the dustie-fute of 'revelry', the acrobat, the juggler
who accompanies the toe-belled jongleur with his merchant's
comic fairground face. He reaches deep into his base latinity,

into his pede-pulverosi from which his French descendants pull their own pieds poudreux. Dustie-fute remembers previous lives amid the plate glass of Les Halles. They magnify his motley, his midi-oranges, his hawker lyrics and for a second Beaubourg words graze Scottish glass then glance apart. In this revelry differences copulate, become more visible and bearable and, stranger than the words or city I inhabit, I reach for my yoghurt and find it there.

SECOND INFANCY

'We've washed her' said the nurse
And then we met a bank of sour carbolic air,
My grandmother hovering in a tiny wicker basket,
A gossamer mesh of rib and hair
Caught on its interstices.

Suddenly I remembered that trip with her
To Greenock, the smack she gave me
For imprinting a ring of muck around my eye
When I pressed it to whorls in the pier,
Trying to see the sea.

And later, on the boat, as I pulled towards me
Her cats-cradle, the game that always made
The shape of her forgiveness,
She kissed me, as I kiss her now.

Looking down through the criss-cross cot,
She seems to gently see-saw
As we did once on disused gangways,
And in the evening light threaded
Between the latticework I briefly see,
Through the dark rings of my eyes, the sea.

PARIS — FORFAR

From the window of the Hardie Condie Café, I see the ghost
of a rich friend of my grandmother drive down Forfar's Main
Street in a Rolls-Royce in which I was sick as a child. Behind
me the watercolours of stick girls walking through trees are
misted blobs percolating in coffee steam. Mother comes in
like Scott of the Antarctic carrying tents of shopping. The
garçon brings a cappuccino and croissants on which she
wields her knife with the off-frantic precision of violins in
Hitchcock's shower scene. Soon I will tell her. Show her dust
in the sugar spoon. Her knife gouges craters in the dough like
an ice-axe and she tells the story of nineteen Siberian ponies
she queued behind in the supermarket. Of Captain Oates who
boxed her fallen 'Ariel'. The chocolate from her cappuccino
has gone all over her saucer. There is a scene and silence. Now
tell her. Tell her above the coffee table which scrapes with
the masked voice of a pier seeming to let in some waters, returning others to the sea, diverting the pack-ice which skirts
around its legs. Tell her a fact about you she knows but does
not know and which you will tell her except that the surviving
ponies are killed and the food depot named Desolation Camp
made from their carcasses keeps getting in the way. From this
table we will write postcards, make wireless contact with
home and I will tell her of King Edward VII Land, tell her of
Hut Point, of how I have been with Dr Wilson and then alone,
so alone, in day-blizzards just eleven miles short of the Pole
and ask her to follow me. I am afraid she has been there already. She smiles like the Great Beardmore Glacier and goes
out into the street with stick girls to the thirty-four sledge-
dogs and the motor-sledges. You are too late. Amundsen is
in Forfar. She has an appointment. Behind me I can sense the
canvases, the dried grasses pressed into their grain like eczema
on an open palm. Later I will discover her diary and what I
told her.

Bob Last

J

Six thirty a.m. Indeterminate scales of grey emerge from the mist as cold rock. Thirty metres up a lone climber clings to crushed and distorted basalt. Steel biceps shift, flex, shift again. For a moment his torso is rigid, chest stomach hips an armature redirecting weight against the cliff. His eyes focus deep within the rock. Beyond his grimaces, or to be precise, behind them, a sleeping city sprawls towards the sea.

Immaculately balanced stone facades bracket a gap site hastily patched with hoardings. A huge billboard proclaims: 'This is yours'. In its shadow a nightwatchman's hut.

A man sits in front of a noticeboard festooned with safety-at-work posters, time sheets, and the slogan: 'McSafe — Security is our Success'. He clutches a mug of steaming tea with both hands and stares at the breakfast show on a television barely an arms length from his face. Shards of glass fly through the air and the last remnants of a window pane slowly keel over and crash to the floor. He makes an infinitesimal adjustment to his posture and changes channel. It's winter.

Marty's Grill was once proudly modelled on an American Diner. *Ad hoc* modificiations in best Scottish hardboard serve to give the place a more homely air. The pattern has been burnished off the formica panelling by years of use, little eruptions of rust mar the chrome, greasy deep pile dust covers the extractor fans. Marty himself looks similarly well used. Maclehose a big, well proportioned man waits for his coffee to go cold. He reads a newspaper. How extensive were the CIA's attempts to destabilise the Wilson government in the 60s?

A Fat Woman sits nearby. A brown man's suit is stretched over her frame, the stiff roll of a white polo-neck props up her jowls, her eyes are obscured by thick lenses, her greying hair is tied back so tightly that it pulls at her skin. A plate laden with black pudding, eggs and beans etches an oily smear on to her newspaper. She catches her breath between mouthfuls, a rogue bean falls onto the Star Bird she has been appraising.

Between time checks the radio host enquires just how important is it that the Iceland—UK gap be closed?

A refuse truck lumbers past the window. Maclehose gets up. He twitches in the Fat Woman's direction, she doesn't reciprocate, but Marty feels obliged to acknowledge the departure of such an esteemed customer. Unfortunately he finds this a difficult task when it is a departure that is repeated day in day out without change in action nor circumstance. 'Aye, it's a day all right.'

Seven a.m. A bench serves as a perch for two boys wrapped up against the cold, a brass plaque indicates that it was discarded in memory of a long forgotten citizen. The boys' gaze is at once distracted and meticulous. A storm has left debris fluttering across the tarmac. Piles of rubbish are arranged at intervals along the pavement. Curious lumps embalmed in plastic and enigmatic heiroglyphs stamped on soggy cardboard hint at a different life behind each door. Traffic signals blink at each other across the empty street.

One boy flicks his red fringe clear of steel-rimmed spectacles, it flops back over his forehead. The other boy talks earnestly. Even at this hour the city radiates noise but, by concentrating carefully, it's possible to make out his friend's words as he terminates the exchange, 'Don't talk.' A refuse truck grinds across the junction.

A red light gleams behind a filthy iron grid, air brakes hiss, the chassis subsides. A song leaks from the cab. The brake light reverts, a door slams, again the shift of weight on the suspension, creaking steel, then nothing but a diesel engine under strain reverberating across the cobbles. J has finished his shift.

A dank stairwell. Rough hewn geometry, the middle ages camping in the midst of modern decay. There's no sharp leading edge to the steps, nothing for a shoe to get a purchase on. J's careful spiral is accompanied by the sound of metal clanking and scraping against stone. Electronic carcasses dangle from each arm. He pauses at the second landing, removes a large padlock hanging unsecured from a bolt, and opens the door to home.

Daylight has not yet displaced the colour flooding in from a street light misled by a faulty time clock. Blistering paper glows orange. An archipelago of eroded linoleum clings to a grid of grime caught between damp boards. A rubbish bag overflows with the empty husks of takeaway meals, flashes

of magenta from a malfunctioning sign on the building opposite highlight a Big Mac wrapper.

In the middle of the space upended furniture supports a
skin of black binliners and thick polythene patched with bold
words: Safeways, Dixons, Frasers, and Wm Low. Droplets of
water have travelled down three floors from a hole in the
roof to lie glistening on the shiny polymers. Piled beneath
them are all manner of televisions, radios and VCRs. Some
are decrepit, barely able to summon a flicker or bleep, some
are brand new, state of the art. Circuit boards protrude from
holes hacked in the casings, makeshift switchgear is embedded
in a spiky morass of wires taped and soldered to every avail-
able connection.

A jumbled alphabet settles down as it scrolls up one of
the screens:

> ... when the jet crossed the road it was only two
> feet in the air. It hit runway lights on the far side
> damaging its wing flaps. Despite being warned of the
> damage by controllers the 707 flew on to Kuwait and
> Bombay ...

On another, white fuzz, and to its left:

> a body suspended by the wrists from a cross will be
> pulled downwards by gravity.

Gravity is penetrated by mathematical symbols. Plus. Minus.
Approximately.

> ... where it changed registration and disappeared. It
> first arrived at Lusgate on Friday under US registration.

A scan line drifts lazily up the screen.

> This produces enormous tension in the muscles of the
> arms, shoulders and chest wall.

On other screens echoes of text are subjected to interference
patterns, ghosting, and equipment that is falling apart:

> The condemned man begins to stifle. This leads to
> metabolic acidosis.

and:

> cash. It took on 130,000 lbs of fuel in two batches.

In the far corner an electric fire struggles to make an impact on the room. A heap of blankets twitches. J crouches to

feel a woman's limbs articulated against the cold. He presses his palm between her legs, the blankets muffle the texture of pubic hair. A lens and flash adjust their position in the light of data reaching them from an autofocus sonar. J catches Carol briefly exposed to the cold and light. A miniature production line squeezes the print through stainless steel rollers, Carol buries herself in the blankets. Behind her two girls cry in soft focus. Tears advance across their cheeks a single scan at a time, fifteen thousand, six hundred and twenty five sweeps of an electron beam every minute.

Nine thirty a.m. A truncated corridor. Greys, creams. Bare fluorescent tubes hang from the ceiling, those that work bolster daylight enfeebled by grime caked on the windows. A portable gas heater nestled amongst stacks of manila folders helps out the central heating. Three people wait on a bench. They have reached an inverse nirvana.

Maclehose ignores them. He clamps a headset on his ear. Though there is a chill in the air he begins to sweat where the black foam encases his skin. The print head of an antiquated electronic typewriter inches across paper marked with prompts, boxes, and borders. 21/1/1985. n/a. n/a. He makes slow progress. Strings of x's suppress every other phrase. His comments spill out of the designated space. Diphenhydramine. The dictaphone jams as he double checks the reference . . .

Two thirty p.m. Blinding white light, motorwinds, shutters clicking. A dimly lit hotel suite emerges between flashes, velour curtains are drawn against the daylight. Men of every shape, age, and size crowd in. They are festooned with cameras. In one viewfinder: foggy flesh tones. In another: fingers slipping between a triangle of fur. A sharply focused spine arches across the field of view then Carol turns towards the forest of moulded rubber, ground glass and machined metal protuberances of the highest possible specification. She moves two feet to the right and the forest sways with her like time lapse film of phototropic seedlings adjusting to the movement of light. What, she wonders, controls these ugly bio-mechanical hybrids? Vaginotropism? Carol kicks off her shoes and ploughs through the crowd.

She emerges into an oasis of grubby calm. This grand hotel has methodically slipped downmarket. She leans back, golden plastic and canvas textured board press into her back. She adjusts the sunny rural scene, one of many that mark out the corridor. The photographers disperse, their glamour course at an end.

Four p.m. J presses against the window of a bus. His breath condenses on the glass and blurs the view of a housing scheme. It is wet from recent rain. Young men clutching air rifles group and re-group on a wide verge, oozing an inarticulate threat. The youngest sport Nike shoes and hooded sweat tops. The older ones wear motorcycle boots, and denim jackets encased in stained nylon waistcoats emblazoned with gothic letters proclaiming 'Death or Victory', 'Triumph', and 'Hot Metal' above neatly embroidered birds of prey.

The bus halts outside a block of flats. Its windows are boarded up. Some, where the first to escape used to live, are grey and weathered, at others garish fresh plywood indicates recent departure. J eases past a door hanging off its hinges into a stairwell littered with abandoned chairs, prams and rugs. J mumbles at a door. He can hear the footfall of a bulky man pacing back and forth.

On the other side a rusting girder wedges the door shut. Brown patent slip-ons with brass buckles, a grey tweed cuff, then a slice of cheek and forehead slip through chinks of light. A woman is lit by a mute television. Cigarette smoke and its soft shadows drift across her grey face and over a nicotine stained eye.

A small packet emerges from the letterbox.

Five thirty p.m. A cavernous warehouse. Maclehose rolls back the heavy door. The distant sound of music. A massive bent steel component snakes across the floor on wooden blocks. Its coat of fluorescent red paint is fresh, even wet. It glows under floodlight streaming through panels in the roof. A huge letter M, taller than a man, lies rusting against the wall. It is made from sheets of steel pressed to resemble solid girders riveted together. An A lies flat, its apex pointing nowhere. An I and an S are entwined in a corner. Maclehose lowers himself onto an X. The music stops. A door opens at the far end of the space. 'Mr Maclehose!' The music starts again. A vehicle swings round the warehouse sending slivers of light across the floor. Maclehose looks up, crates covered with serial numbers, and fragments of the decrepit alphabet are caught in the beams.

A corrugated iron canteen is tacked on to the end of the warehouse. A band plays in a space cleared of tables and chairs. Bright lights fail to enliven grey-green, grey-brown, grey-white and just plain grey. A not so secret admirer of Elvis puts his heart and soul into an old song. 'Your good thing, your sweet, good thing.' Maclehose takes a seat. 'Is

about to come to an end.' To his left a pressed tin ashtray, to
his right an empty beer glass, in his hand a bottle. The song
continues, 'Everything that's good to you . . . ' He drinks.
'Ain't necessarily good for you.' If Maclehose wasn't Maclehose he would weep into his beer. Elvis is unaccustomed to
having such an effect on his audience, he plunges on.

Carol pulls a chair up to Maclehose's table and looks at
the band, the ashtray, then Maclehose. He turns to betray a
confidence, 'Kodak, Ilford, Fuji, they're all making money.'
Their eyes meet, 'You make money, the hotel makes money.'
He pauses, 'I'm keeping it moving, whirling it about, stopping
it from laying siege. We don't live in castles up above the
action, down here anything that doesn't move falls apart.
Calculate, estimate, even pray for a good guess, because believe you me that point where you're gaining on things, that
point when you're stepping out in front, it's moving, sashay-
ing along the X and Y axis, pirouetting way up ahead.' He
stares at Elvis, 'and its the dancers who inherit the party.'

A phone booth nestles against a concrete wall designed to
keep out either the ocean, or the Third Reich, but now redundant in the middle of new land. J's pocket is weighed
down with coins. Undeterred by nightfall a huge mechanical
digger relentlessly fills in the sea by the light of tungsten
halogen filaments. J looks towards the canteen where Carol
and Maclehose are dissected by irregular window panes set in
rotting frames. He puts a coin in the slot. A car glides by
within inches of the phone booth. 'At the third stroke it will
be five forty precisely, at the third stroke it will be five forty
and ten seconds, at the third stroke it will be five forty and
twenty seconds, at the third stroke it will be . . . '

Eleven p.m. Street lights reflected in gleaming silver bum-
pers reveal a car built when chrome didn't have quite the
same strategic status. J stares through the Capri's rear window. He is uncomfortably aware of the effort of seeing. The
more he is aware of it the more his vision slows down, the
more focus becomes indistinct and depth intangible. The
passenger leans towards him, 'How you doing?' J shrugs, his
lips begin to form words but he thinks better of it. 'Nothing?
Fuck nothing!' J still does not respond. 'Your fucking problem . . . ' The passenger tails off as he realises he is none too
sure what J's problem is. He turns to the driver, 'You want to
know what his fucking problem is?' He doesn't. A car jumps
the lights behind them. Blurred colour rushes across J's field
of view and when small islands extend within his depth of

field they pass by before he can observe their form, rather than their mere presence or absence.

The passenger doesn't abandon his analysis. 'You remind me of ma wee sisters, they were always pretending, mostly Americans, when Ma's fridge was full ... ' The driver switches the radio on, a voice lists the weekend's events. The passenger is undeterred, 'They'd sit in front of it, Ma's high heels danglin off silly wee ankles, crossing and uncrossing their legs, maybe wiggling a wee bit and talking about "their" swimming pools, like they were being interviewed for TV. The fridge had to be full though or else they didn't feel American.' There is no response. He turns to the radio, 'Aye that's it, talk shite.'

Eleven fifteen p.m. The Europa Bar, a tacky joint rented out tonight to an itinerant nightclub. The sound of a bass drum pounds the air at one hundred and twenty beats per minute, the snare drum sounds like it was recorded in an aircraft hangar. Lights carve out a fabulous new world with every beat. The tribes styling on the crowded floor are oblivious of the silvered and flocked wallpaper, the brass, Caribbean-style wall lights, the expanded polystyrene mouldings glued to the ceiling. Other cliques huddle in the humid zone surrounding the dancefloor, their feet stick to carpet encrusted with the layered residue of evaporated lager.

In one corner plastic rubber plants have been pushed aside to accommodate a large television. J absorbs the deluxe glow: shiny guitars in close up, singers slipping through golden fields and agonising on lonely beaches as they run towards carefully selected lenses, the sense of being under fire re-created with lasers and lamé, all cut to rhythms at disorientating cross purposes with the pulses reaching his ear.

He edges round the periphery through conversation after conversation. His route attaches Frank's reply to Karen onto a question for Davey, Spike's confidential revelation onto Rab's insult. J pauses in front of the Galaxion machine, his face illuminated by yet another alien demise. Across the room overworked bar staff ensure they project an appropriate air of indolence. In between, the crowd and Carol dance. Empty flesh and bones pumped full. Limbs, muscles, slits curving across the beat, carving up space.

Midnight. J descends stone steps to a sub-basement. A large wooden door encrusted with weathered paint opens onto a narrow earthen floored corridor. Forty watt lightbulbs hang from bare wires strung along the ceiling. Centuries of

building, demolition and re-building on foundations clinging
to steep slopes have left a complex of silted up cellars and
basements. Each room re-excavated by an enterprising tenant
is less and less well defined, some are interconnected by door-
ways, others have arches at hip height and stairways termin-
ating at the ceiling.

Cables bound with greasy tape pierce the corridor at knee
height. J stoops to pass through another doorway. The passenger is huddled between towers of tape labelled 'Rendez-
vous with Anne' and 'The Resurrection of Eve', 'Insatiable'
and 'Inside Desiree.'

In the next chamber J can barely see Maclehose's bulk
lurking in the gloom. The image of a naked man turned
three quarters away pierces the dark. 'Hello J.' Maclehose's
comfortable monotone. He takes a long drawn out breath
through his nose. The buttocks slip a few lines downscreen.
'You think we've got something to talk about?' Maclehose is
so still, and it is so dark, that J could forget him if it weren't
for the fact that his head rotates from side to side causing
his glasses and the saliva on his lips to catch the feeble re-
flections of the fleshy screen. Anyway he doesn't really seem
to be speaking for J's benefit. 'Maybe.' J. waits. 'Maybe.'
J already feels guilty. It seems to take at least a minute for
the glasses and the lips to rotate left, away from J, and then
back towards him. 'Everything is negotiable.'

J waits for just such a negotiation.

Twelve twenty five a.m. A large saloon in the middle of
the road, engine running, lights burning, empty. A boy presses
his ear harder against the grille of an entryphone. J walks past
bright shop windows where microwave ovens are treated like
divas and humble suitcases like stars. Nothing moves except
two girls who gaze at every deep gloss display. One wipes a
tear from her eye.

J is overtaken by a desire to run. As he picks up speed
the speed itself generates fear. He stumbles and swerves, a
gloved forearm and pastel skinned elbow swish by, a cuff-link
glints above a jacket pocket. He glimpses eyes set in skin
painted verdigris, a rose, and, as he regains his balance, dark
suits silhouetted against a sparkling matrix of foyer lights. He
scuttles past a car showroom, past the melodramatic splen-
dour of this year's model then turns a corner into mono-
chrome calm. A young man with cropped hair, filthy donkey
jacket, shredded jeans, and baseball boots flits past on a skate-
board.

Twelve forty five a.m. Water defies gravity by flowing up a television screen in J's flat. Light from passing cars sweeps across the ceiling. Carol tenses, touching her chin on a scaffolding bar wedged across a doorframe.

J turns on one VCR, then another and another filling the room with words. Eustasy, eutectic, and Euthymol. Azygous. Azioc. Apple.

Carol lowers herself from the bar, 'There isn't any difference.'

J continues to assay the flickering entrails. A ballroom washes across his retina, bright sunlight bathing a girl dancing alone. Beautiful male hands break bread onto dove-grey marble.

Carol tries again, 'Nobody's heart aches.'

Crumbs float past a sparkling glass of water. 'This,' a gravelly voiceover pauses dramatically, 'is yours.' Mottled yellow letters glide to the left where they huddle together in the corner of a screen.

Carol nuzzles J. 'No one's.'

She stretches back amongst the cables and monitors, opens her coat and eases faded sweat tops across her stomach. Her fingers trail across her ribs. Fabric gathered in her hands brushes against her nipples. She glows white against tartan lining and dark leather. A ripple travels across her skin as it confronts the cold.

The beautiful hands are breaking bread again on the screen above her.

The layers of sweatshirt slip back. Carol pulls hard at thick tights, pauses, then pushes down over her hips, stretching her arms to their fullest extent, 'Let's sweat blood.' She reaches between her legs, crushing cotton against herself.

Words reflected in a window drift across Cassiopeia and Ursa Minor. A vertical hold isn't holding.

SAFEWAY 8969 SANTA MONICA BLVD	
02/16 5.24PM STORE 129	
CUST 282 REG 5 OPR 132	
GROCERY	1.39*
ARROWHD WATR	1.09*
PISTACHIOS	3.99*
KNIFE	2.19 TX
2.68 LB @ 1/1.39	
XLG TANGELO	2.65*

```
PRODUCE                    4.49*
MINUTE MAID                1.09*
1.26 LB @ 1/1.39
RED PLUMS                  1.75*
   TOTAL              18.85
   CASH TEND          20.00
   SUBTOTAL           18.64
   TAX PAID             .21
```

PLAY WIN FOR LIFE BINGO

Maurice Lindsay

LIVING BY WATER

What makes us want to live beside water,
the looking-glass of space, the vacant eye
that stares the sun back at its own blind game?
Fretted, we say it scuds or suds with laughter,
but, raging in destruction, wonder why
the difference of touching wears no name.

So we make friends with it on our own terms,
searching dry land for the world's regard —
the which, if we can find it, proves to be
a temporary bind against the harms
that eat away the fabric of reward,
like termites, or the washing of the sea.

Salty or fresh, blocked ice, revolving rain,
water retains its own identity,
mimicking moods and seasons by the way,
as thought dissolves into itself again
and we stay land-locked in sufficiency
till death froths off the surface of our day.

Peter McCarey

CASTLE OF INDOLENCE
(Keep in a Cool Place)

First sweat dries to a crust in the breeze,
breaks up on the second, like the backwash
of a wave, pushed back on the shore by
the next one, seasick.

You leave the novel like a tepid bath
and everything's where you left it
the old iron bath of yourself
with the novel and all its crew
foundering in you, your gastric juices.

I was reading like a tourist too long,
and all I wrote was like postcards home.
Now the next time I write,
you're going to turn the thing over like an
overhead cam, a mechanical stone, and say yes, but

GASTARBEIT

It's arriving in a foreign place at night
when you don't know where to go
you see your small self and the
compartment in the window
the luggage rack and houselights floating by
fluorescent rooms, and it enters you,
and the cold of its indifference to you
lodges like a virus in the ghettoes of your blood.

THE MEMORY OF THE MIGRANT SCOTS

I   Flow

It starts in transient souls and cells
It's stored, potentially, in the machine.
Switch on. What turns the disc and fan
lights up the VDU and may obscurely
corrupt your cells electro
magnetically hardly (Geiger)
counts as national
in any hoardable way the wind
turbines the clouds the rain comes
clattering down through dams
Namibian metals rot at Dounreay
the coal at Seafield. We worked there a
mile out under the sea and on Sundays
or whenever the day off was, I don't remember
what he said (remember it, remember! that
's what this is FOR) we took the bus or we
walked and we sat there on the sea cliffs in
Fife and we looked at the sea we looked at the sea.
When a man died down there his mates
would keep him down until the end of the shift
so the widow would get his full day's pay.
So the management
brought in a doctor
to ascertain the time of death
and that was when he was paid till.
From the Highlands and Ireland
from Poland and Lithuania. They worked outwith
their majesty's tidal sway neither on nor under
the land. This isn't blood and soil,
nor yet a notion
grounded in shared speech, says one whose forebears
came up the Clyde on a bike.
Terroni who took ship — the Anchor Line,
I guess, for New York —
and landed at Glasgow. Paddy's Milestone,
Ellis Island; the Statue of Liberty? well,
it's like on a peace march to Dunoon a friend of mine
accosts this Marine and says to him look,

if you have to have your rotten missiles
why can't you keep them somewhere safe,
in the middle of nowhere? and he says 'Lady,
I'm from Brooklyn; believe me,
this IS the middle of nowhere.'
There speaks a man who's sailed with Palinurus.
Aye, my education's Roman but my values
are the poor and pushed about's, and I've no
time for Trojans bearing title deeds.
This is for those who were born here and left
it's for those from elsewhere who've come here
it's for those who've passed through if
they've brought a sign, a song,
a child, a church, a tune,
a film or building,
dance or language,
a programme, an attempt,
come ON, a response!

Kenneth MacDonald

THE NORMAL BROTHER

With Sidney and me it was always that way. At school, at
home, even in marriage, it's always been him, him, him.
Sidney and his brother. Mrs Johnson's other boy. The boy
with the brother. I'm not saying he was favoured, that he
looked for more attention than he was due. It just came to
him naturally because of the way he was, once they found
out about him. And once they did, I was second best, un-
interesting, in the shadows, as sure as if I'd been put into the
background of a photograph while Sidney sat at the front.
Oh sure, my parents told me not to worry about him getting
some attention, that it would pass in time and it was just because people were that way, and I should be glad of the
contribution a member of the family was making to society.
But it never did pass. And it wasn't a member of my family.
It was him, my only brother.

The phone's dry burr pulled me out of sleep. Like a drunk-
ard, I stumbled through to the kitchen and tugged it off
the wall. Looking at the oven clock, I could see it was 2.17.
Outside I heard a car coming down the drive and knew the
headlights would reflect through the curtains in a second or
two, illuminating everything in the kitchen like a lightning
flash.

'Hello?'

'Hello, Mr Johnson?' A man's voice, urgent and business-
like.

'Yes.' There's the light, brightening up everything for a
moment.

'Mr Johnson, first allow me to apologise for disturbing
you at this hour of the night. This is Dr Marks, at the Lawrence Infirmary.'

Right then I knew what this was about. Right then I
should've interrupted the doctor, told him of his error, given
him Sidney's number, and gone back to bed. But the voice
on the other end was insistent and passionate, like a man
determined to be heard. And before I had the chance, he

went on.

'I know we've never met — I understand it's usually Dr Rodgers you've been contacted by in the past, but he's in the United States at the moment — but we have a little problem here that I'm afraid only you can be of any help with.'

Again I could have butted in, but my initial irritation at having been woken was being replaced by curiosity. Curiosity to hear the things I'd been denied, the respectful, deferential tone I'd never been accorded, the confidence I'd never been party to, all because they wanted Sidney, and not me. I decided to let this doctor ramble on for a bit yet before I told him.

'As I say, I can only apologise for the lateness of the hour, but we've only just been notified ourselves. Matter of fact, she's not even arrived yet. But they've told us the helicopter's on its way. I'm afraid her condition isn't good, Mr Johnson, which is why we had to contact you right away.'

I pictured the scene at the hospital. The sudden realisation of the patient's urgent plight. The search for the right person who could help. The efficient manner in which that person had been located. The surgeon striding purposefully into his office and closing the door behind him before picking up a telephone. Maybe a cigarette for his nerves. Nah, not a cigarette, he was a doctor after all. You never knew, though, with those guys. There was a silence on the line.

'Mr Johnson? Are you still there?'

I realised I hadn't said anything since picking the phone up.

'Yes,' I said, 'I'm here.'

'Ah, good. So, um, would it be possible for you to come down here as soon as possible? I really am terribly sorry to have to ask, but I suppose that you'll know that these things always seem to happen at times like this.'

Here's what it's all about. My brother Sidney has this rare kind of blood. There's something in his cells that hardly anyone else has, and for that reason, he's allowed to give blood only to people who have this same type. That's why they wanted his blood and his blood only, and that's why he always got special treatment. They first found out about him when he was about seven years old. I'd be about ten. We were out playing on the old tree which had been hit by lightning at Wishart's barn when he fell and cut his head. I remember that by the time they got him to hospital he was

was covered in blood, although he hadn't cried or said he was in pain. So they took him in and gave him a transfusion, but he just seemed to get worse. No-one could figure out why. They were giving him A or B or whatever group he was, but still he was ill. Then they screened his blood and found out that his cells contained something special, something different from the blood he was being given, and the normal blood was causing a reaction. After that it was plain sailing. They gave him some kind of universal plasma and after a few weeks he came home. He wasn't any different, but everything else was. I was told not to excite him or hurt him, that he wasn't as healthy as me. 'Poorly' was the word my mother used. It took her years to get over it. At night my brother and me would hear my parents talking low, and my mother would always talk about Sidney turning blue when they'd given him the wrong blood in the hospital. She went over and over it, as though she was trying to exorcise it from her mind. When she talked about it I looked across the darkened bedroom at my brother, but he'd just lie there, staring at the polystyrene tiles in the ceiling above him, not showing any sign he could hear what was being discussed.

They've needed to use Sidney's blood about eight or nine times since they found out about him. I suppose there must be other people who are like him and need the type of plasma or rhesus factor or whatever he has that makes him so special. When he was about twenty he found out what it was that he had in his blood. Some doctor had told him and even given him microscope slides, one showing his blood cells, and one showing normal blood cells. Although we didn't have a microscope to look at them, my mother inspected them for hours. She prized them. They never looked to me like anything but identical splodges of brown paste. Sidney himself never seemed to bother much about his condition. We've never really talked about it, him and I, but after he married Linda she told me he was very matter-of-fact about it, and treated the calls for another pint of blood as part of day-to-day life.

Hospitals watched him like a hawk. They kept careful records of when he'd last given them blood, when he could safely give more, making sure there was plenty of time between each visit. For some reason I never understood — my mother explained it to me, but, to tell you the truth, after a while I didn't really listen when she started talking about it —

they couldn't stockpile his blood — couldn't freeze it up and take it out when they needed it. They had to get it fresh, like vampires and virgins. I said that to him once, but he didn't see the joke. Linda said I was sick. Once one of the hospitals had to send for him in an emergency to save a man who'd been hurt in a train crash, only a week or two after he'd given some blood. They treated him like royalty. They kept him in for three days afterwards for observation and told Linda to report any signs of tiredness, anaemia, or loss of appetite when they let him go home. But Sidney never complained or showed any signs of being either up or down due to having given blood.

At school, Sidney always used to get extra milk — 'to keep him strong' — and if he fell in the playground or during a football game, it was a red alert. I was sent running home to tell my mother while the teachers worried about whether to send him to hospital. Four or five times there was this terrible scene where I'd come dashing back to the school with my mother and Sidney would be sitting in the headmaster's office, sipping from a china tea-cup, dried blood on his leg or his nose or somewhere. My mother would burst into tears and the headmaster would try to calm her down, Sidney would say he was alright, and I'd stand there feeling guilty and ashamed, red to my ears. And of course there were some kids who went out of their way to give him a hard time, punching him and scratching him with nails so he'd bleed. He never said anything about this to my mother, knowing what a fuss she would make, but one day she saw some marks on his neck and got the story out of him. After that I'd to chaperone him everywhere. She even told him not to go to the bathroom at school unless I was with him. It got that bad.

I hung the phone back up and went through to the bedroom and sat on the bed. Outside it had stopped raining and the streets looked quiet and new, as though no-one had ever walked in the puddles before, or disturbed the tangled webs of the trees' leaves. I put my clothes on slowly, enacting to myself doors being opened in front of me, brisk handshakes, thanks, more apologies, quiet empty corridors, the musty, disinfectant smell of old hospitals, men in striped pyjamas with bottles of orange crush beside their beds, snoring softly. I fished out my only white shirt and put it on.

Of course when the interest began — in Sidney's mid-teens — he lapped it up. He didn't say anything, but I could see he was enjoying every minute of being at the centre of attention, being important, being in a position where he could've — had he wanted to — manipulated people. I remember one occasion when some baby was born with a blood disorder and they sent for you-know-who to save its life. It was touch and go for a while but eventually the baby pulled through and Sidney was big news. They had TV cameras and everything. The newspapers were full of photos of him and the baby, with the parents, and so on. I even got to be in some of them. I was about eighteen or nineteen. The one my parents still have, in a yellow-cream coloured frame above the mantelpiece, is from one of the Sunday magazines. It shows Sidney and me photographed in our garden, him smiling cheerfully at the camera, me looking down at him the way the photographer had told me to. Underneath, the caption reads, 'BLOOD BROTHERS. Sidney Johnson, the fifteen-year-old with the life-saving blood, pictured with his "normal" brother, Steven.' That just about summed everything up. They didn't even ask how to spell my name.

At times, I wondered whether, beneath that eager-to-please image Sidney presented, he ever used his uniqueness to his own ends. Was his humility and resigned air a device to mask his own selfishness? I can recall incidents when it seemed to me he invited special treatment — causing a fuss if he cut himself and things like that. But generally, I don't remember him abusing his luck, certainly not so he could profit over me. Most of the time it didn't seem to interest him, and he certainly didn't talk about it unless asked. I suppose it might've embarrassed him, being known for being out of the ordinary. Maybe it still does. The last time I saw him, at New Year, we were in each other's company for two days and the subject was never mentioned. I got the impression it was something he and Linda preferred not to dwell upon, something they'd blanked out of their minds, not to be discussed except in privacy. I wondered at the time how they could be like that, knowing within themselves that the call would come again, sooner or later, disrupting the pattern, bringing it into the open once more. The burden of having to consciously ignore Sidney's condition, then have reminders of it persistently appear, must have been a strain to them. I sat back in the taxi and considered, probably for the first time, the burden that had been placed on my brother and sister-in-law. I wondered whether they regarded it as a gift, however

many lives it saved, however grateful the authorities and re-
cipients were. But within myself, outsider as I was, I knew
Sidney's blood was a blessing, something special. And there
in the darkness, with the rain outside sparkling the streets
like a fairy tale, there was the suggestion that anything might
happen at the end of all the journeys that passed me by and
which were taking place as I travelled, including my own;
that endless possibilities of any kind might become capable,
limitlessly so, but only to people who had been honest and
good.

James McGonigal

RAISE YOUR HATS, GENTLEMEN

Well settled here on the brow
of the hill, do you not find the sky
fits us like a bunnet

or more like whole hat-racks of them
— ten styles at least for each season
and maybe six for the time of day:

the cloud-flecked grey tweed, dampish to touch,
the blue with white tassel, that is worn at a rake,
the orange and violet weave of sunset tartan

or a brown with funereal trim
for late afternoons in November. High winds
blow them away, but always

throw us another, as easy a fit —
even the black and white checked cap of winter,
moth-eaten and draughty.

On this northeast slope, our head of leaf
thins and falls early. But each daybreak we raise
our hats to the bunnet maker

and admire in the glass his choice for the day.

RESURFACING

Cobbles like fossil mushrooms
push through tar. The folk who lived here

screamed their Scotch abuse, bit flesh
and shook with cold. We are changing

the world: distant from each other
where can we live but close at hand;

saving our strength to fight new wars in air
we put each crisis into autodrive.

At six, drift home to microwave and drier
that hand us suits of waterdrops to wear.

The news says hunger, and the sea is higher.

LIVING BACKWARDS

1

My fingers touched yours as we passed the babies
to each other: busy hands make a kind of August
breathing — grit and flies, pine needles, a runner
panting through woods to find the taste of brown
loch water that has drawn him lies
almost beyond strength. I failed the test,
falling backwards to the sound of stage thunder.

2

Swallows transcribed quick Arabic curves in air
but sang in Persian: contest and echo
dripping from roof-ridge and cloud;
midsummer hogmanay in the beech tops, you'll never
sing alone. We waited for winter
to stiffen in chest pains. With strips of indigo
gales lashed the back and sides of the house.

3

When I held your nape as a reader at noon
cradles his book in one hand, and drinks, each day
spun like a churchyard scene where mourners' tears
dance the grave dizzy. Handwriting stopped
suddenly as rain when that high voice the moon
spoke from her cloud; and we came at last to stay
in each other's life for years and years.

Alastair Mackie

PARISIAN SONNETS

1 At the Place des Abbesses

Seated on a bench I watched the housewives
on their errands in the Place des Abbesses.
To my right a wino cat-naps and strives
against the chilly light and drowsiness.

Suddenly from the Metro shaft appears
his bench-mate and boozing crony. One foot,
slowly, then the other, as if he fears
the ground would yawn again and he would shoot

downwards into the chaos of DTs,
a jerky puppet. He tries out his tongue
to greet his partner but no words arrive.

All night he sucked an empty, now he sees
a bottle on the bench. The cork's like a bung.
He gropes for it and pulls it to survive.

2 Hitler's Children

We came down to the ornate dining room
and sat down. They emitted a silence.
It was weighty, impending like a doom.
It hit us like communal violence.

Their German began. The coffee was done.
No one moved. You went to replenish it.
We served ourselves. It was despatched to one
the most rabid of mouth, who let it sit.

He was the fuhrer who led the chorus —
first grating German, then brutish laughter.
We could only sense we had a virus

sitting in our midst, still breeding after
Dachau, Treblinka, Mulhausen, Auschwitz . . .
We too were smothered in their laughing fits.

3 Beggar in the Metro

Baudelaire's 'Parisian Pictures' live on.
I saw in a tunnel in the Metro
an Algerian beggar, both eyes gone,
clinking his begging bowl, while to and fro,

a distant river, Paris, seethed in spate.
She had no eyes for him who had no eyes,
who kept his chosen pitch early and late
and turned his stitched-up pits for charities

that seldom dropped into his needy bowl.
He had the patience of those who depend
on mere chance for eking out from day to day

a life, that waits for some casual dole
to earn a living, from what strangers spend
out of their heartless magnanimity.

4   Near Pigalle

We saw three black transvestites in a street
that sloped its way down to the Rue Pigalle.
They seemed shy novices fresh to the call
to serve the community's sexual heat.

They sat on doorsteps equal yards apart.
Above their thighs a swatch of red cloth tried
to be a mini-skirt that could not hide
this makeshift caricature of a tart.

Too muscular their legs, their torsoes bunched
with unenticing breasts a clown might flaunt.
Upon their heads a slipshod turban drooped

and hid one eye. In this tatty gear cooped
up between the door-posts where each hunched,
they hawked their wares to buyers on the hunt.

5   In the Metro

French conversation was a mitrailleuse
firing its fusillades about our ears
everywhere we went. Of that foreign bizz
I could make nothing. All these six long years

at schoolboy French left me illiterate.
But once inside the Metro all talk died.
Through the swaying dark the narcotic rate
of the wheels held the atmosphere tongue-tied

as if spell-bound in a tense eeriness.
Was this a vestige of something devout?
It had the throbbing silence of a church.

Some sat mute, others gathered in a press
of bodies near the door, as they made out
light, whitening the darkness with a lurch.

6 *Madame La Tortue*

Each morning with drugged steps and slits for eyes
the Algerian servant brought breakfast,
coffee and croissants. Each step seemed her last,
so slow she shuffled as if an early rise

and the big coffee pot had drained her strength.
Her lips would struggle to loosen a bonjour
as she paced herself on her snail-slow tour
of the room to meet the challenge and length

of the marathon to the kitchen . . . Yet,
one night on desk duty, no longer set
in her sluggishness, kohl staining her eyes,

she moved her body with a supple poise,
Irish green top, bobbed hair as if she knew
she was the belle, not Madame La Tortue.

7 *Place du Tertre*

We climbed the leg-weary butte of Montmartre
debouching on the easel-crowded square.
Forgers were copying Utrillo's art —
his mason-work on the architecture

of Paris, street by peeling street. Flake white
mixed with plaster . . . walls; Sacre Coeur's domed breast
and nipple . . . blank perspectives under a light
drained, melancholy, as if dispossessed . . .

We sat outside a cafe and drank beer
while Utrillo's hack heirs touted their skill
among the tourists. A head in charcoal

500 francs . . . How did the place appear
Bastille Day, 1914? Outbursts of leaves fill
the empty square. Far off, tiny figures stroll.

Hugh McMillan

OPEN DAY NIGHT

Forging south
while the storm snaps at our heels
and cars drift by on tongues of spray.
In the slough beside the motorway
lorries are anchored to flat vistas
of grey and green.
The road has drowned
and in a monotony of rain
we are becalmed
while trees and buildings slip by,
filling with wind like sails.

Near Crawford the bus gives up.
Willie gets out to blow down the tubes,
scrape away the calluses of brine,
coax it that final thirty miles.
Near a knot of workmen
brown with engine oil
I unload our cargo of schoolgirls.

In sight of these sleek and wiry men
with eyes like hot rivets,
starved of female company
since they were marooned here
at breakfast,
the girls light up like lamps,
unload the morning's intellectual suet
like mad balloonists cutting ballast loose.
They are alive.

The bus coughs to a kind of life
and heaves away from the racks of tyres,
the dead plants, the trellis work
like rigging,
Willie and I laughing like old salts,
too loud,
and the girls in the back
quietly dreaming of the sea.

ON THE POINT

John Gordon is dreaming,
unfurled like a flag on Ardtornish Point.
His family came here
on holidays, parking their lozenge
of a caravan near needle cliffs,
in the lip of the gale,
only a toehold, a stone jammed
in the wheel, from disaster.
He dreams of his mother, legs laddered in light,
who barred the debtors' door
and swept up the summonses in the morning
in a small green tray,

of his father, who used oils thick as thumbs
and left a black trail
like a comet's: the sharp spines
of paint rearing like beasts,
the photographs in Palestine
astride that great horse.
Lawrence of Dumfries.
Whatever faults or virtues the pair of them
had owned John had forgotten,
if he ever knew,
and bared down to symbol, to private myth,
they stare like Errol and Mrs Flynn
from endless fields of Kodachrome.

John sniffs, as tiny boats hop
like sandflies in the slough of sea.
The more anchored he becomes,
the more he seems to see his wake,
the more he hears birds squealing
like chalk on the wall of sky
and sees the sun sweeping boys back for tea,
when they didn't need to dream of summer.

Gordon Meade

THE SEDATED

Sedation makes them
Easier to handle, calms them down.
They glide across the ward's
Polished floor carrying their shelled heads
Like snails with hangovers.

Their eyes are sunken
Pools. They don't know what time
Of day it is, what month,
What year. Their cotton-wool brains have been
Saturated with chloroform,

Their threadbare veins
Burnt clear with morphia. At night,
The nurses bring a medicine
Cabinet round the ward on wheels. A dozen
Plastic cups, a dozen cures.

Their mouths close on
The holy tablets. Sleeping, they feel
No pain. In their dreams, they
Are circus performers — tumblers, acrobats,
And clowns. They wake up
With their heads in the lions' mouths.

THE SPILL-WAY

Staring into the water
Of a man-made loch, looking
Into its folds of black,

And searching for a stone,
Is like looking for a star
On a cloud-filled night.

For a moment you think
You see one, and are mesmerised
By the sight. You want to leap

Into the loch, wrap yourself
In its cloak of darkness and sink
To the bottom, a stone yourself,

Be visited by the nibbling
Lips of salmon, the healing scales
Of tench. But then, your vision

Drifts an inch from that spot
Of total inaction, and finds the rapids —
Six feet of churning water that races

Like a pie-bald pony down
The spill-way's gaping mouth. You see
A leaf stuck on the pony's flank

Rush past and, in the flicker
Of an eye-lid, disappear. Slowly,
You come back to your senses

And thank, your eye-sight's
Fly-like hovering, and your instincts'
Fish-hook grip, on fear.

THE SCRIMSHAW SAILOR

In the belly of a ship
On a storm-tossed sea, a sailor
Carves out the figure of a polar bear
From the jaw-bone of a whale.

Delicately, with cut-
Throat razor and sail-maker's awl,
His nimble fingers etch in the pupils
Of its eyes, the talons on

Its shaggy paws. Outside,
The ocean batters at the ship's
Stout timbers as the tempest blows.
Inside the ship's dank hold,

The man becomes, himself,
A scrimshaw sculpture, fashioned
In the sea's own image by the ship's
Thrown pitch and tumbling roll.

James Meek

RECRUITMENT IN TROUBLED TIMES

The torturer had written to me at the office, suggesting a place and a time for our meeting. I knew the bar well. It was at the top of the High Street, not far from the ruins of the Kirk Saint-Martin. The Kirk had not always been ruined. A leaking gas main had blown it to smithereens some months before. I knew just what happened because I saw the hand-out McWyvis from Propaganda wrote for the gas board to distribute to the press. The truth was that the explosion had been the work of an English suicide bomber. His rucksack had been packed with home-made explosive. He just had to pull a toggle and it went off. We supposed his intended target was the Marischal's tower house in the Castle walls, but once the bomber started running over the cobbles his heavy boots let him down and the gendarmes were able to take him out. He pulled the toggle before he died, and the church had the worst of it. A few days later a wee boy found one of the terrorist's hands floating in the Nor' Loch.

They knew exactly where to come when they needed someone to interview the torturer. But then I wouldn't work for the security service if it wasn't a well-run organisation. There's little point in sounding off about the demonstrators and agitators and perverts and English sympathisers if you haven't got an efficient outfit of your own. Some of the boys the Bureau takes on these days are very smart, and they cotton on straight away. They can see it's not the ideas of the terrorists and protestors you have problems with, it's the sheer disorder of them, the slipshod way they go about things. You wouldn't mind them chanting Scots Out Scots Out if only they'd do it in unison, if only they'd drilled it right. You wouldn't mind the dyed hair if only it was the same colour and the same length and they looked after it properly. That's what's so frightening, it's not the opposition versus government, it's chaos against order.

But even the best of these new Bureau recruits, when they look at us old hands, they think you can get people's

respect for the organisation just by spit and polish. They think
it's all in the gleaming boot, the razor-creased trouser, the
shiny belt-buckle, the mirrored sunglasses. They think it's in
cultivating an emotionless stare, in knowing how to ask people
to remove their clothes or account for their sexual activities
without betraying the least hatred or disgust towards them.

Not so, I tell them. Och, these things are important. But
what really counts is the paperwork. That's what makes
people respect the Bureau. That's what gets them reporting
for interrogation when they're asked, and in an appropriate
state of anxiety, too. The secret is not to let forms pile up
in front of you. You process them immediately. If some
random suspect fills in an ordinary interrogation form lazily,
and misses out a few details, you don't shake your head over
it and put it in the file with the others. You send it back
immediately by express courier with a big red stamp on it
saying INCORRECT — ONE WARNING ONLY WILL BE
GIVEN. That's the kind of efficiency that pulls the ordinary
citizen up short with a hollow feeling in his stomach if he's
wavering on the edge of a political misdemeanour.

But people get the idea an efficient security service is
only bad news for the agitators and the terrorists. That isn't
the case. It can be hard on the people who work for it as
well. In a tight ship like the Bureau, there's no room for
ambiguity about your function. Each department knows its
duties, and its duties are known. I happened to work in Personnel. There was no question of uncertainty about whether
our department should interview the torturer. It wouldn't
have done any good for me to complain that it should have
been Interrogation who did the interviewing, although they
were the people who were going to make use of the gentle-
man in question. It was all set down in the Regulations for
the Conduct of the Scottish Bureau of Internal Security, the
1965 version: 'In the event of physical force being required
to encourage a repeatedly recalcitrant subject to divulge,
for the welfare of the majority of the body politic of the
Federated Commonwealth of Scotland, France and Canada,
information believed with just cause to be held by the said
subject, it shall be the task of a senior member of the Bureau's
Personnel Department to recruit a suitably qualified and experienced member of the public to perform in relation to the
said subject the necessary acts of physical force. "Suitably
experienced and qualified" may for the purposes of this pro-
vision be taken as appropriate descriptions of candidates with

at least five years practical experience in allied trades or professions, such as surgeons, dentists, butchers and PT instructors. In the case of fishmongers the required period should be extended to ten years and should include experience of aquatic mammals such as dolphins.'

I couldn't argue with that. There wouldn't have been any point. There was no time anyway, because we needed the torturer very quickly. The Englishwoman Hepforth was being held by some very nervous gendarmes in a squalid and unsuitable cell in a station on the border, near Pontefract. As soon as we could get someone to do the necessary work they would be able to sign the form and have her transferred to Edinburgh. Otherwise they'd have to release her within forty-eight hours and she'd vanish into the rabbit-warren of London.

I'm proud we work under such tight restrictions. People who complain about our methods have no idea of the procedures we have to go through even to arrest somebody, let alone keep them in custody. They imagine we can walk into homes without warrants, drag any old suspect off to Craigmillar, keep them there as long as we want and rough them up at our leisure. Sometimes I wish it were that simple myself. But the fact is that our every action has to be accounted for, documented and filed. And that's got to be the best way. It will always be hopeless for the Bureau to try to justify its actions to everyone outside the Bureau, but it is necessary for the Bureau to justify everything it does to everyone inside the Bureau. Hard and distasteful tasks can only be made acceptable by imposing such rigid and immensely detailed codes of practice on them.

All the same, I can't deny it was with some reluctance that I acknowledged my duty of interviewing the torturer. The 1965 regulations specified a senior member of my department, but there were many others of equal or greater seniority to myself. When I asked my supervisor, Roxton, why I had been picked, he said only that confidential procedures laid down for selection had been properly carried out. I explained that a glance at the salary scales showed the torturer would be appointed at a relatively high grade, and would be earning more than myself, which surely made me insufficiently senior. Roxton said the torturer was only to be employed on a temporary basis, and would have part of his pay docked if a subject in his care failed to divulge the required information before entering a non-living state.

I then went too far, suggesting to Roxton that instead of

employing a torturer, a certain amount of leeway should be allowed the Bureau's everyday interrogation staff in their methods. When he didn't interrupt, I elaborated. I pointed out that as long as we allowed Interrogation to deprive subjects of sleep, blindfold them, give them minimal amounts of food, shine bright lights in their eyes, strip them and put them through intimate body searches, it would be quite reasonable to permit the occasional slap, kick or mild electric shock, simply to encourage them to appreciate the seriousness of their situation.

This went down badly with Roxton. Though he was a small man, in his early sixties, he had a loud voice, and the glass partition dividing his office from the rest of our floor vibrated as he shouted. He was astonished, he roared, that I should suggest the use of physical force on subjects by anyone other than qualified experts. This was Scotland in the twentieth century, not medieval Germany. What would the President say if he thought the Bureau had licensed itself to beat up members of the public when and how it liked? If pain had to be administered for the good of the Commonwealth, it had to be done carefully, in stages, by someone who knew enough about what they were doing to write a detailed report afterwards, explaining what happened, and, if need be, why the subject's body had ceased to function at any particular point.

Towards the end of his outburst he calmed down, took off his glasses and began cleaning them with a cloth from his top desk drawer. Adopting a gentler voice, he gave me the address of the torturer I eventually contacted. As I wrote it down, I asked whether it might not be a good idea to take the man onto the staff permanently.

Roxton replaced his glasses and frowned. The torturer was well past retirement age, he told me. But if the man could recommend a successor, perhaps something could be arranged.

On the night of the interview I discovered I was to have a partner, a junior clerk from my department. It was not explained to me why, or whether he would have a role in the conversation. His name was Beaumont. I was not best pleased to have him along. I did not look forward to him listening in to the interview, waiting to see if I made an obvious mistake, or else butting in as the torturer was answering a complicated question. Besides, I had consoled myself in my unhappiness about carrying out the interview with the thought that I must be respected by my superiors in Personnel, if not highly thought of, to be given such a delicate task. To be accompanied by someone else put the issues of status and responsibility in the realms of doubt. For once I felt the Bureau's efficiency had lapsed.

I met Beaumont in the car park after dark. We shook hands. He was pleasant enough, but his age worried me. He was only twenty-five. As we walked towards the car I noticed he walked strangely, not exactly with a limp, but with a certain hesitancy in his step.

The car was in my name, an unobtrusive black Ramsey sedan with the white-wall tyres then in fashion. As Beaumont reached for the door-handle an automatic pistol fell from his waistband, clattering onto the tarmac. He bent to pick it up.

'Sorry,' he said. 'Should've got a shoulder holster, shouldn't I.'

'You shouldn't have signed a gun out at all,' I said. 'We work for Personnel. We interview people. We don't shoot them.'

'Sorry,' said Beaumont.

'Put it in the glove compartment, and leave it there.'

Rain began to fall as we hit the Northern Autoroute. By the time we reached the Holyrood exit it was coming down in torrents. I was glad. The fewer people on the streets the better. It was said the English preferred to fight in the rain. I didn't believe it. Even terrorists liked to be warm and dry, especially when they were setting their incendiaries.

I eased the car up the glistening cobbles of the High Street. The lights were all against us. I pulled on the handbrake and offered Beaumont a cigarette. He refused.

'Been with the firm long?' I asked.

'Twelve months,' said Beaumont.

'Enjoying it?'

'It's what I've always wanted to do.'

'What did they tell you about tonight?'

'It's an interview. The firm needs someone to persuade a terrorist to give some information.'

'How persuade?'

'I don't know, something about physical force.'

'Torturer. You've got to say it, you know. You might as well get out now if you can't accept what's got to be done for the good of Scotland.'

'Aye, torturer, all right. I just wanted to make sure I was

using the right words. I've had my balls chewed off for saying "bugging" instead of "electronic surveillance". I'm not worried about what's got to be done.'

I pulled up on double yellow lines opposite the bar. There was no need to be too discreet in such a heavily policed area. A gendarme approached as we got out of the car, his face half-concealed by the veil of water dripping off the peak of his kepi. He told us to move. I looked him in the eye. Some of the juniors in my department think the Bureau's field agents can make the flics recognise them just by doing that. I was glad it wasn't true in my case. If you could do that you were bound to stand out in a crowd. I had to flash my badge. The gendarme shrugged insolently and walked away. It was depressing that the best efforts of the Bureau could be rendered useless by the slovenliness of these uniformed morons. Luckily for him his waterproof cape covered up his number, otherwise I'd have put in a report.

Before we entered the bar we heard a loud mechanical throbbing above our heads, drowning out the sound of rainwater running down the gutters. We looked up. Only a few hundred feet above us in the night sky floated the President's airship, manoeuvring towards a mooring at the Castle. The throbbing increased as the pilot put the propellors into reverse. The immense machine swung gracefully into position and began firing lines at the waiting airmen on the battlements.

Beneath the thistle of the Presidential cypher on the fabric of the airship's fuselage, a line of cabin windows glowed. I could make out little of what was going on inside, but no doubt it was the regular complement of weekend guests, being lavishly entertained at the nation's expense. Usually they would take off from Linlithgow on Friday evening and head for a sheltered corrie in the Grampians where they would dance and drink champagne through the night. In the morning anyone who was still conscious would grab a rifle, lean from a window and take pot shots at any deer unfortunate enough to be grazing down below. They would spend the rest of the day cruising around the Highlands before returning to Edinburgh for the obligatory tour of the Castle. The Marischal had to make a show of welcoming the guests. Who knows what he and his officers really thought of such intrusions. I did not have access to the Bureau's secret reports on relations between the two men — reports which no-one save the Bureau would ever see — but like everyone else I had heard the rumours. Everyone in Government service pledged an oath of allegiance to the Commonwealth, to Scotland and to the President. We in the Bureau were no different, except being the Bureau, our oath was classified. It's enough to say that in the order of the oath, the Commonwealth and Scotland came first. What if the President's ancestors had been first over the barricades when the mob stormed the Tolbooth in 1790? That cut no ice with me and probably cut none with the Marischal so long as the President was up in the clouds in his gin-palace zeppelin, a Parisian tart on one arm and a stuck-up Quebecois floozy on the other.

Such thoughts as these disturbed me deeply. It was not so much the contrast between the Marischal, standing stiffly to attention on the ramparts, and the drunken rabble the President would lead to meet him. Contrasts were easier to resolve. It was the link between the Marischal, myself, and the Englishwoman Hepforth that I found difficult. We were each sober, dedicated, disciplined individuals. Yet the Marischal and I fought against Hepforth and the others of her seemingly indestructible cadre for the sake of so many sloppy, unthinking idiots, just as the admirable purity of her passion for English independence was spoiled by the gang rivalry and racketeering among her supporters.

We entered the bar. It was empty, a low-ceilinged, split-level place lit by dim yellow globes. The floor was thickly carpeted, muffling sound, like the lobby of an expensive hotel. Beaumont followed me to a table at the back, where a mullioned bay window looked out on the ruined Kirk. I ordered a pastis, Beaumont a whisky.

'You don't look comfortable,' I said to Beaumont.

'Should I take my coat off?' he asked.

'Up to you,' I said.

'I'm taking mine off.'

'Well, I'm leaving mine on.'

Beaumont scowled and turned the lapels of his coat up. He did not take it off.

'I could do this job, you know,' he said.

'That's no way to speak to a senior officer,' I snapped.

'Well, we're equals here,' said Beaumont.

'What the hell do you mean, equals?'

'I mean we've both got an equal chance, haven't we?' Beaumont cleared his throat. 'You surely didn't expect me to sit here and let you do all the talking?'

I drew in breath to raise my voice, then exhaled and

frowned. What was he talking about? I was too old to have to take these crazy juniors under my wing. We looked at each other in silence for some seconds. At this point the torturer arrived.

Still confused by Beaumont's words, I got to my feet too fast and held out my hand to the torturer before I really knew what I was doing. As we shook, his watery grey eyes stared out of their red sockets into mine. I must have registered alarm; my hand, thrust out at first with instinctive eagerness, must have flinched within his grasp. He knew I did not want to be touched by his fingers. I could see that he knew, and realised then that an efficient torturer would learn nine-tenths of what he needed to know from nine-tenths of his subjects long before the necessity of inflicting pain arose.

Beaumont pumped the torturer's hand firmly, smiling the earnest, puckered smile offered to those who have made noble sacrifices for the greater good.

As we sat down our drinks arrived. The torturer asked for a beer. He looked to be well into his seventies. His thin head of silver hair was slicked back with oil. He seemed hunched but strong under his tweed jacket.

Nobody spoke for a few moments. None of my usual opening questions applied. 'Tell me what you're made of,' in particular was a can of worms I had no desire to open.

The torturer looked at me and Beaumont in turn, his natural expression a gloomily downturned mouth, slightly open, with just the faint suggestion he might begin to dribble.

'Well,' I said. 'I understand you've had some experience of this kind of work.'

'Once,' said the torturer, 'they took me to a room in the middle of a security compound in Hertfordshire. A man sat in the corner with his hands handcuffed behind his back and his feet tied together. Two sergeants from army intelligence had tried to question him about the liberation movement, but he had said nothing. They had beaten him. By the time I came to him, his face was bruised and swollen and some of his teeth were missing, but he had told them nothing. I told the soldiers to leave the room. I sat him in a chair and gave him a drink. I showed him what he looked like in a mirror, and laughed with him about it. We talked about his home town for a while. Then I explained to him, very gently, that I had come to make him suffer great physical pain for a more or less indefinite period. I explained the various methods I would use, and pointed out that once I had begun I would not necessarily stop, even if he made a full confession. I patted him on the shoulder, and told him it was about eleven in the morning outside. I said I would go for a coffee in the canteen, then come back and begin torturing him.

'I left the room. I went to have a coffee and read the morning paper. I came back about fifteen minutes later and went into the room, closing the door. The man had his back to me. I walked over and touched him on the shoulder. He gave a spasm and died, without a sound. I don't keep a count of the number of cases I deal with. It has been more than a hundred. Up until now only that man has died at my hands.'

I glanced at Beaumont. His face was shiny with sweat.

'I can imagine how a man could die on you like that,' said Beaumont, his words emerging all in a rush.

'Can you?' said the torturer.

'Yes. Eh ... you were only doing your job,' Beaumont went on. 'I mean, I think ... it's the biggest challenge of all, isn't it? There's loads of hard men in the Bureau, in the field and in Interrogation, who think they're the ultimate tough guys when all they know how to do is knee and punch and chop and shoot. They haven't got the guts to sit down and, eh, just do the business. Like you do. Because you've got to overcome your natural instincts, I think, to do it cold. Torture people, I mean. I mean you're giving up everything, so much anyway, to find out this information. Anyone can risk their life, but you risk losing your family, your friends, all for the survival of peace and freedom. That's the way I see it, anyway.'

The torturer supped his beer. 'What do you think?' he asked, nodding at me without looking in my direction.

'I regret the necessity for torture,' I said. 'I don't envy you your task. I would much rather it was possible to extract such information from people by means of drugs or hypnosis or electronics. Sadly such methods have not yet found favour with the Bureau. Within the scope of using pain to coerce informants, however, I believe there are good torturers and bad torturers. Are you a good torturer?'

'How would you define that?' asked the torturer.

'A bad torturer likes inflicting pain for its own sake. He is a weak man who enjoys making people who are physically and mentally stronger than himself suffer. He knows what he is doing is wrong, and enjoys it all the more for that. A good torturer dislikes inflicting pain on anyone. He is a weak man who has been shoved into the job by people who are mentally

and physically stronger than himself. He knows what he is doing must be done, and that gives him the strength to carry on.'

'For God's sake, let's not get too philosophical,' said
Beaumont.

'Keep your voice down,' I murmured.

'OK, OK, just let's not get too philosophical. It's a job that
needs doing, a tough job, the toughest, but straight-forward. A
good man will do it because he knows it needs doing and because he knows there is no surer, more direct way of rooting
out the subversives who are trying to bring this country to a
state of anarchy. I mean, Christ, it's obviously a hellish thing to
do, but someone's got to do it. I'd do it. I'd do it carefully, and
not mind how long it took. It's that or innocent people dying.'

The torturer nodded slowly. 'The crippled torture subject
who suffers agony and nightmares for the rest of his life is
the disfiguring scar on the face of the nation, restored to
health after successful surgery.'

'Exactly!' said Beaumont.

The torturer straightened his mouth at the corners. 'You
don't mind a little philosophy when it comes from me and
not your colleague, I take it.'

A clear point scored over Beaumont. I smiled. 'You
haven't answered my question,' I said to the torturer.

He turned his eyes on me for only the second time, and
even then with obvious reluctance.

'It occurred to me several years ago,' he said, 'that the
existence of physical pain was one of the simplest and most
useful clues there was towards the nature of humanity. Pain
is a real, definite thing, the most real and definite thing there
is. And yet no scientific laws can quantify or explain it. We
have access to pain to the very last instant of our lives, when
all else is finished — food, drink, passion, coherent thought.
Pain is an inexhaustible and ever-accessible human resource.
But why? Why should the signal which warns us of danger to
our physical well-being cause us to suffer? Why not red lamps
in our eyes, or tiny sounds within our minds? There can only
be one reason. Humans are fundamentally careless, lazy and
stupid, not just to each other but to themselves. Our creator,
or the evolutionary forces which shaped us, made a being so
hideously self-destructive that it would ignore any warning
of danger to itself that did not cause it to suffer directly and
immediately. So we received the gift of pain. Not wee blips
of pain at a constant level, telling us to check if something
was wrong with us. Not a limited number of zones of pain,

confined to crucial areas of the body. No, our nature is so staggeringly reckless, so incredibly foolish that we possess bodies brimming with the potential for pain, overflowing with pain, so much pain that most of us cannot keep it suppressed for more than a short time without it breaking out somewhere, even when we are young.

'If you believe that the cause for which you torture is just, these facts are a consolation. I see my subjects as I see myself: one part reason and nine parts pain. By the time I meet my subjects, the reason part has already been approached and provoked, and has failed to respond. You could compare that to a man who can feel with his tongue that his tooth is rotting away, but does not visit the dentist. If his tooth did not begin to hurt him, he would leave it until one day the tooth dropped out and was lost forever. But it does hurt him, and for that reason he is forced to take action to save it. Unfortunately we have not been created with any similar inbuilt mechanism when it comes to rotten ideas and mental errors. So it is sometimes necessary for pain to be inflicted from outside, to alert subjects in the only truly effective way to the danger they are in. That has been my task.'

'Right!' said Beaumont. 'Right all the way.'

'All the way?' said the torturer.

'Makes perfect sense,' said Beaumont.

'What I've said is an equally good argument for an English terrorist cadre to torture you, if they captured you.'

'Argument's got nothing to do with it where those bastards are concerned. They don't have to justify themselves to anybody.'

'How about God?'

'They're Protestants. Protestants and God don't mix in my book. The way I look at it, the Pope's with us, and if the Pope's with us, I'm not going to argue with him.'

Instead of replying, the torturer took out a crumpled, snot-stained handkerchief and blew his nose half a dozen times, wiping carefully after each snort. Beaumont watched every move he made, fascinated. I imagined the torturer's clients watching him in the same way, as he broke off his work to perform this and other humdrum acts of personal hygiene. It occurred to me that once the torturer began his work the pain he transmitted would have a powerful momentum, capable of carrying it through such pauses, indeed making such pauses essential in not dulling the subject's senses with a continuous application of suffering. As the

subject gazed at the torturer blowing his nose the mental anguish he would feel, wondering how long his respite would
last, would more than cancel out any relief experienced at
the brief cessation of pain, and would create a torment
indistinguishable from the effects of the torturer's actual
physical work. I was sure the torturer would apologise
politely to the people he was torturing for breaking off to
blow his nose, and again before recommencing, and wanted
to confirm this was so. But for the first time in twenty years
of interviewing, the question died before it reached my lips.
I did not want to sound like Beaumont, eager to discover the
practical heart of the matter of torture. I remained silent,
allowing the torturer to continue his dialogue with the junior.

'Do you not feel it's necessary to have a wee bit of a
rapport with your subject?' asked the torturer.

'No!' said Beaumont, laughing an over-hearty laugh. 'No
way. That can't be realistic, surely. No. Laddie!' He called
the waiter over. 'Same again, will you. No, let's face it, you've
got to really feel something against anybody you torture.
And to me there's something wrong with the bulk of the English. I mean they're not exactly bright, are they? They drink
too much, they can't cook, they're mean and they're violent.
And they're always ready to take our handouts. If they knew
what was good for them they'd be glad to be part of the
Commonwealth. Like you say, if you need to make a few of
them suffer you're only saving them from themselves.'

I was about to regain control of the conversation, and
had begun to speak, when the torturer cut in, still ignoring me
and addressing Beaumont. I began tapping my glass on the
table in annoyance — a weak and petty gesture which served
no purpose. I stopped and held my peace until the torturer
finished.

'What makes you think it'd always be the English you'd
be working on?' he asked Beaumont.

'Well, that or English sympathisers. Traitors I'd call them,
and mostly Protestants. There's nothing lower than a Scot
who sides with the terrorists.'

'Could you — ' I began, before the torturer interrupted
me with a wave of his hand.

'Hold on a moment, sir, if you wouldn't mind,' he said.
'We can talk shortly.' He stood up. Beaumont immediately
followed suit. The torturer put his hand on Beaumont's
shoulder and firmly pressed him back into his seat.

'These are troubled times,' the torturer told Beaumont.

'Too troubled for those who see the struggle for order in terms of Scotland and the Commonwealth versus the English liberation movement. The struggle goes deeper. It is a struggle of calm against violence, of sobriety against overheated passions, of abstinence against indulgence, of neatness against untidiness, of normality against eccentricity, of law against anarchy, of responsibility against recklessness, of obedience against rebellion, of custom against innovation, of maturity against delinquency, of fidelity against depravity, of resident against itinerant, of permanent against transient, of average against extraordinary. Mr Beaumont, it is not a struggle of loyalty against loyalty.' He took a deep breath and turned to me.

'Could I see you alone, outside?' he asked.

I hesitated, but realised that to refuse would finally reveal to Beaumont my uncertainty as to why he was present. I got to my feet. We looked down at Beaumont, who was forlorn, pale and angry in his raincoat with the turned-up collar.

'I didn't get it, then,' Beaumont said.

'I'm afraid not,' said the torturer.

I followed the torturer outside. The rain still fell heavily. We sat in the car.

'What's going on?' I said. 'Beaumont seems to have got it into his head that he was in line for your job.'

'Yes,' said the torturer. 'Unfortunately his mindless enthusiasm for torture as a career prevented him getting it.'

'I still don't understand, I admit. It seems to me there's been an appalling cock-up somewhere. But I'm happy to recommend you as the Bureau's man for the Hepforth job.'

'Thank you. You know I used to work for the Bureau, once upon a time, as an ordinary staffer.'

'Your record doesn't show that.'

'The one you saw doesn't. It doesn't say I'm English either.'

'No. You don't sound it.'

'I left a long time ago. I grew tired of the hypocrisy. If the English really wanted independence, really desired it, there's nothing all the Commonwealth could do to stop them having it. Instead they work within the system and get sentimental about the past and blame the Scots for their troubles. It's left to a few fanatics, brave and ruthless fanatics if you like, to actually do something about it. The English are sanctimonious about the Bureau and the way it operates. It's easy for them. They don't know how lucky they are. There's no administration that doesn't breed some arm like the Bureau.

Supposing James IV had lost, and the English had taken Scotland and France and all the rest? To hear some of them talk, it would have been the perfect state. Law and learning and brotherly love for everyone. Don't you believe it. They would have sprouted their own bureaucracies and secret policemen. They would've had their own special cells with straps on the chairs. They don't know how lucky they are. Or maybe they do, which is why most of them put up with being citizens of a province.'

There was a commotion up the road. I switched on the wipers, partly to see what it was and partly to delay a number of important and worrying questions I had to put to the torturer.

Further up the road there was a sentry box, in which one of the Marischal's guards stood stiffly to attention, his rifle held diagonally across his chest. A woman was dancing around him, very close, hitching her white satin dress up around her hips, and singing or shouting something. Her skin was white, whiter than the dress, her hair was black and shiny, her lips wide and red. The guard did not move or change his expression. A little distance away stood a man with a champagne bottle, in dishevelled evening dress. He was watching the woman dance around the guard.

'Only a few people know what is best for them in these days,' said the torturer. 'Men like us are needed to give a sense of certainty. Soon someone will cut the moorings of the Presidential airship and it will drift off into a storm with him and his Cabinet aboard. They will disappear in the gales off Stornoway, and the wreckage will never be found. That is the time that the greatest certainty will be needed, and the strictest justice enforced.'

'How did you become a torturer?' I asked.

The torturer clasped his hands in his lap and bowed his head. 'I was working as a senior officer in the Bureau's Personnel Department,' he said. 'One day they asked me to interview a prospective torturer.'

There was no sound for a time but that of the rain drumming on the roof. I too clasped my hands and bowed my head. I thought of making a lunge for the gun in the glove compartment, but I am not the kind of man to cause trouble.

'I wouldn't be a competent torturer,' I said. 'I'm not suitably qualified in terms of the regulations.'

'There are other regulations.'

'I haven't seen them.'

'They're secret.'

'But I didn't even know they existed.'

'If you had known they existed, they wouldn't have been secret.'

'What if I refuse?'

'Don't refuse. You're a single man. There's a very attractive salary and pensions package, you get a free house, eight weeks paid holiday, police protection and private psychiatric treatment. I've studied your profile. You've already begun to torture people in small ways. When you interview job candidates you make them suffer unnecessarily by leaving long silences after they have finished answering. You hint to them that you know of indiscretions in their past which might warrant Bureau investigation whether they get the job or not. You did these things with Beaumont when you interviewed him. In fact I'm sure you wouldn't mind torturing him again, in a more concrete sense, something you might well have to do one day if he doesn't wise up to the shakiness of the Commonwealth he worships so fervently.

'Also you run the risk of being tried and punished before a secret tribunal if you turn the job down. The Englishwoman Hepforth is already on her way to Edinburgh. She was released in your name, on the assumption you would accept the post. If it turns out you haven't, you will have committed a criminal offence.' The torturer turned and leaned towards me. He took gentle hold of a lapel of my raincoat. 'Besides,' he said, 'there's something you don't understand. I'm not fond of my job. I don't mean I think it's wrong, I'd just rather somebody else was doing it. What you have to realise is that no torturer starts from scratch. There is a chain of us, stretching back into the past, an unbroken chain of torturers who have brought in the next generation to take over their jobs. We can't give up until we've got someone to replace us. I don't know where the man is who recruited me. He may be dead. But I am not going to risk him being alive to carry out the threat he made to me should I retire without leaving a replacement. I can't, do you understand? Do you understand?'

The torturer's voice had become high-pitched, and his grip on my lapel had tightened. He was shaking me.

'I understand,' I said.

'Do you? Do you understand? Torturer on torturer, back thousands of years, always looking over their shoulders for the shadow of their predecessors, always with an eye out for a new recruit to take over the burden. I can't let you break the chain. I can't. You're it now, you've got it. I'll be watching you.'

That was how I became the Bureau's torturer. I realise now, as I stand preparing for my first job, the degree to which he misled me. I try to think of myself as the impersonal administrator of a necessary, useful, alerting pain, but this is not possible. I realise now how quiet a matter the torturer made it sound by quoting the one example of a subject that had died before torture began. I don't doubt all the others screamed until they were hoarse and their lungs ached. Hepforth has a strong pair of lungs. I have asked for a hood to cover her head. If only she knew I am as much in the dark as she is. Of course I cannot tell her this. In the end, Beaumont was right: for God's sake, let's not get too philosophical. I do not care, as I spark the crocodile clips to test the current, whether I am a good torturer or a bad torturer. The old man is looking over my shoulder. He has put the terror in me. I just want to pick through as many layers of Hepforth's agony as I have to, as quickly as possible, until it is finished and I can get on with my search for a successor.

W.S. Milne

STATION COTTAGES, PORTLETHEN
(for ma sister)

The auld psalms, Frances, mind,
at the brae's fit, aneth roddin,
whicht roses, the shuggly haathorn —

the kirk wi its sma-like steeple,
soor goosers niver eaten,
the caravan some thocht queer
whaur moths were aewys sleepin,

thocht brings back in order?

The standin-pump that caad up forkies
as weel as watter wi ivery pail,
the water-butt that bent the licht,
airn pans derk as nicht
whaur buckies biled, thocht brings back

grun lang since turned.

OCTOBER

Diamant-sherp the air, sae bricht the sun
you speir for aipple-blassam,
and in your hert drifts
    the bitter tang o haathorn.

Stane-dry the rowan, in low licht
split cane scores the horizon.
The haill warld seems teemit,
    ivery step back-answerin.

Aroond, wheesht. In the gaitherin wind
frae the back o beyond, frae gairden and fairm
the fa o bruckle leaves, jist. It's summer,
    cauld, and deid.

Michael Munro

SMOKE

It was a cheap dining table, round, topped with white formica, sporadically stained and marked with scratches that defined themselves in ineradicable dirt. Its legs were shiny silvery metal tubes bent into squarish curves. She sat at the table, a beer-advert ashtray, overloaded, straight in front of her, hedged in by her cardigan-clad forearms. Lukewarm winter afternoon sun through the streaked window picked out a white strand or two amongst her short reddish hair. She sat there smoking, tautly, determinedly, biting off each drag, holding onto the inhaled smoke as if she grudged to let it go. The fingers holding the cigarette shook continuously. Her long legs were crossed at the knee and one instep tucked behind the other ankle. She didn't look up, over to where he slumped comfortlessly on a straight-backed dining chair.

His back was to the light, his head turned to be able to see from this only window. His look was almost desperate, as if any minute now something wonderful, maybe even someone with arms full of rescue would swim into view in the middle of Cathcart Road. His sole movement was an occasional smoothing of his black moustache with finger and thumb.

He was waiting for her to speak again but she wouldn't, not yet. Her say was over, strong stuff while it lasted, and now it was up to him. Without having to look at her he could feel her silence exhorting him to speak, make reassurances, restitution, resolve everything in a sudden form of words. The different lies, half-fictions and palliatives that made up his usual exchanges with her in this mood were not going to do; that was clear. What was it she wanted to hear? What could make her feel better about this, ease her back into wanting only to keep this thing of theirs going a little longer? He couldn't clear his mind. One day at a time, Sweet Jesus, ran some song's line in his thoughts' chaos.

He was certain he still wanted her but this kind of pressure, this showdown mentality was definitely not needed. The original purposes were being lost sight of. If only she would start talking again it would give him cover to come up with a way out.

She was looking over at her coat and bag, dumped on the tatty couch in front of the electric fire. Just that one step or two, lift them and be gone, into the hall and down the darkened stairs, through the close and out to the light. Easy done. And the car sitting there, escape at the turn of a key, and no turning back. Her foot pressed down as if already gunning the engine. To get away, get clear, be home, in her own flat's calm warmth, in the circle of her books and music. She'd never belong here.

An ice-cream van was circulating somewhere, quite a distance away. He could just catch its tune, some stupid Italianate jingle he couldn't have named. His mind was opened to this sound from boyhood, this overture to cones and ninety-nines, getting raspberry on it, licking the greaseproof paper when the contents were all gone. It must be like that for his own boys. Ian at least was old enough to heed that call, running out of the front door and down the garden path, a pound note clutched like a ticket for the world. The thought of home stirred him into concentration. How long did he have? He was taking Ian and his pal to the game this afternoon. He wondered if he could risk a look at his watch. Would she see, realise he was keen to get away? He observed her closely, waiting until she was caught up in the routine of lighting another cigarette, then without moving the rest of his body he angled his wrist until his watch's dial was visible. That was okay, another hour at least. Sit tight.

It was all right for him to sit there and fidget. Of course, time was precious to a principal teacher with a family and a big house in King's Park to maintain. Why couldn't he say something instead of lounging there glowering out of that stupid window for all the world like an unrepentant third-year boy being lectured. An overgrown boy was just what he looked like, in his designer tracksuit and running shoes. He must tell Her he goes jogging when he comes here on a Saturday morning. It was neat all right; the perfect explanation for coming home half-knackered and wanting a shower. He was that polished; it was all thought out. Back he would trot to home leaving her to cursorily tidy this gungy room and kitchen he'd found for them, to be handy for him though she paid half the rent. Was the odd evening or weekend day's use worth the money? She was getting too old for this, and too old for anyone else, of course. Damn these fags; what must she smell like?

He would have to get on with it. By the time he jogged back to the house, grabbed a shower, got the lads organised, it would be pretty tight to make it to the ground, get the car parked . . . It was all there now anyway, or as much as could serve for an opening. He'd got a few lines sketched out in her silence. Here goes nothing.

'Listen. I'm not interested in giving you a baby. I know you're saying there'd be no demands on me, but I'm not one to dodge responsibilities. I'd still be its father, and I've had enough of fatherhood to do me.'

She sat there, immobile, sun-caught smoke writhing above her head.

'Didn't I tell you at the start I wasn't going to leave her? You knew that, you agreed to that, and not one thing has changed as far as I'm concerned.'

She was rasping a bitten thumbnail on the striker of her matchbox. The noise irked him unreasonably and he made sure of controlling his temper before going on.

'You know, the last fifteen months have been really special for me. I was as good as dead, stuck in an idiotic rut, boring myself and everyone I came into contact with. You were a breath of fresh air the minute you walked into that staffroom. I couldn't take my eyes off you and you knew it, didn't you? Of course you did; you could see through me from the kick-off. Still do. And I've never been much good at disguising how I feel. What's changed? I still feel the same, that we can love each other only and truly for as long as it lasts.'

He paused, but her face gave him nothing.

'Look, nothing's guaranteed in this world. You make the best of what you get. You can't go back to the shop for a refund. We've all got only the one three-score-and-ten and we owe it to ourselves to get the most out of it.

'If you could just drop this nonsense; say this is just a pointless falling-out and we'll get back to the good warm feeling we've always known. Because I don't know what I'd do if you packed me in. If I had to go back to that old life having lost you part of me would be killed. But it doesn't have to be like that. It'll be good again. Why don't I say I've got a conference coming up and we'll go up north for another weekend? What do you say?'

What she said was nothing. She hardly showed that she

was aware of his presence. He tried a last appeal, one that had
borne fruit before.

'Just say you love me. Say you'll not leave me. Please.'

Her move. He sat, still half-leaning forward, as if tensely
awaiting her response, savouring the relief that was breaking
free inside him. He had broken the silence she had imposed
and said what he wanted to say. He hadn't cast anything up
or given any excuse to renew hostilities. The more he had said
the more he had been imbued with a virtuous strength. She
was obliged to respond in some way. Any way would do, just
so she would emerge from that mute shell of wrongedness.

If she made concessions, said something positive to give
him a way back in, then he'd won. Things would go on as
before, in an arrangement that suited him fine. If she was
negative or started that shouting again, maybe even stormed
out as he'd seen her do before, he'd still have won. If this
thing had to end then let her end it, let her be the wrecker
and he the injured party. He could play on that forever.

In many ways he would miss her but in others just as
telling he would be glad to be free of what threatened to
degenerate into just another obligation, one more eater of his
time. And then after a decent interval, if he felt the need
again, maybe something else would come along. He waited
almost greedily for her to open her mouth.

She didn't lift her eyes to his face. She seemed to be
drawing her strength together as she stubbed out her cigarette
in sharp jabs into the little mound in the ashtray. Her voice
when it came at last was jagged with the smoking and emotion.

'Shite,' she said, 'you shite.'

Two tears ran down her face, leaving tracks in the make-
up. Her shaking fingers wiped them brusquely away, then,
grasping the crumpled packet, took out another cigarette.

JENNY IN THE ART GALLERY

She runs from room to room
or rather, toddles at the run.
Slaps damp palms on sudden glass
at stuffed beasts inside.
She names them, once and for all.
A tiger is a dog; the grizzly bear a teddy.
She sings her song and giggles
at her reflection's dance.
The polish of these floors
is tricky for a first encounter.
Surprisedly skating, she shouts laughter
into cool museum silence
and echoes from high ceilings egg her on
to scream full pitch.
She's too high now; best take her out.
A chase past the Anne Frank exhibition,
no time to take it in.
Outside, the wide summer air
a breath on a cool face.

Thom Nairn

SHOUTING AT HARBOURS

The stone rain on a still pool.
Bird's sound on claws in the sand.
Dead fish heads, coral, slate, cold voices.

Gulls and clothes whiplashing
Quiet cars away
With the cold slush of waves.

The small and white dead crabs
Are irregular smears
On the wet leather-black rock.

Nearby,
Men are shouting at the harbour,
Dark, slick and not listening,
Stone faced.

Worlds won't move or
Adopt accommodating forms
For men's voices.

But still, their boats bang as bones
Against the quay endlessly.

WORDLESS

It was always with you then in the later days,
The discursive diagrammatics of motion,

The meticulous precision of your armchair's table,
Always the methodical struggle,

Geometric, systematic and stable,
The moving of that arm by the sleeve.

It's cigarette to cigarette, match to match,
A transport of flies by the ants;

One dead arm, one arm live,
One passing one, limp sleeved to its place,

Your eyes no longer follow,
You have no need to watch;

There the anger cuts deep,
Denied the course of its wants,

Anger stalks in the summer heat,
With you as a shadow in light

Where no shadow should fall.
Dark in the eyes, one dead arm, one arm live,

Always with that methodical struggle,
With too many wordless things to feel,

Here there are cuts too harsh
For any tongue to heal.

ACCOMPLICES

High up on the side of a long, low hill,
The old woman sits on a roughly crafted rock,
A fragment from maps of older people's schemes,
Ahead of her in the widest, deepest space,
The valley runs away in waves,
The early night sky's as red as the sea.

She makes putty of her face,
Dough-pale and dark shadowed, shifting
In her still kneading and needing hands.
Even dead dreams are not so easily shaped
Or as meaningless, but her eyes have a star's fire.

Her elbows, crackling joints, form sharp angles,
Even her spine has something to say,
And her long, wide, cheap skirts billow around
Her wider hips and thighs like a quilt.

She stares along and down the lines of her body,
Teeth and mouth and face as tight as shells and colder,
Coaxing only wild expressions only you'll find:
For months and months she's come to sit here
And no-one knows just what it is she thinks.

Still we can all see that every day
She grows and grows more like the long, low hill
On which she sits.
Angles, crackle and poise are slowly erased,
The soft down on her face catches the cool glaze of moss,
Her own back merges with the vestiges of crags.

Their whole worlds reach to each other and mix.
It can be guessed
Her heart is cut and gouged
As moors for peat, for light and heat
And that she loses, forges and forgets the world
By becoming it.

FUN-TIME

Stooping eyeless over a cake,
The knife handle, loosely,
In shaking, veiny hands.
He uses sponge for balance here,
Well, it's his 95th year.

They spoke and posed him,
Imposing different directions,
In his baggy tweed suit
His warm and heavy boots
Assured a tired balance.

'Close your mouth grandfather'
'Close your mouth grandfather'
They all said this and said this,
'Close your mouth grandfather'
'Your mouth grandfather, close it'.

So he closed it,
He closed it tight
As they all said 'smile',
They said 'smile' 'smile' 'smile'
They said 'smile'.

He did it once with his mouth
And sat,
Said nothing more that day.
This is what comes
Of leaving your jaw undone
The day they have your birthday party.

William Neill

THE MILLMAN

October's moon over the evening yard,
rumble of wheels upon the rutted road,
breaking the earth for all the frost was hard
under that iron load.

Steam tractor, threshing mill and caravan,
come there to part their straw and chaff and grain,
the final fruiting of the peasant plan,
reward of labour's pain.

Into the firelit room the millman came,
with a hook for a hand, a face as pale as death;
the child, who saw all grown men as the same,
drew in a frightened breath.

The millman only grinned and waved his hook,
stuck down his corpse's face to the boy's head:
I'm more alive, my laddie, than I look.
It's just my hand that's dead . . .

and buried too, for it was never found
when the engine skidded on the bank and fell.
I often sit and think about that hand,
waiting in heaven or hell.

MYXOMATOSIS
(Or ... 'The Final Solution')

I saa a puir daft beast the ither day
craalin aboot the park. It didnae ken
whit wey tae shift an wesna feart o men,
but cam up til me wi een bleart an blae.
Thir mappies are a plague the fairmers say:
gie thaim a bite an it will niver enn
till they hae stairved the sheep an kye an then
we'll be sair fasht tae scart a leivin tae.

Ach weill, the enn of rabbit copulation
is fouth o bawties aa aboot the bit,
gizzlin up gress an heizin mankind oot.

Thare's a great swall in human population.
Hou tae mak shair the best yins get tae eat
will shuin finn some wyce new repone, nae doot.

SILLER DREES THE WEIRD

The faut, Dear Brutus, isna in oor staurs ...
up tae a pynt. Thare's naebodie wad say
plittert at pairties till the brek o day,
gaun tae the grewhoonds, bletherin in baurs
an spennin siller on big roostie caurs
is whit ye'd cry the straucht an nerra wey.
Ye's get nae faurer tho, wi praise-an-pray,
I wad opine altho nane ither daurs.

The sterns o some, for aa Wull Shakespeare screivit
ootshine in magnitude the lave; tak tent ...
dinna be fankilt in saturnine rings.

A siller spuin in gub, ye maun believe it,
progs aw yir sterns on tae a brichter glent.
Tuim pooches is whit maks us underlings.

YON BODIE FRAE PORLOCK

Doverin bi the ingle, Samuel thare
wes glamourt bi his harns in opium dwaum
o damsel, dulcimer an pleisure dome,
an *earth in fast thick pants* but tae his sair
scunner, a chapper heized him frae his chair;
we're tellt a nauchtie neebor-bodie cam
in yon wanchancie hour tae wauken Sam
wha hained a blaud or twa, but tint a quire.

Hou aft wi ithers it has happent sae:
juist whan the gowden lyric shaws its heid
some drapper-in gars ye pit doun yir pen.

An whan ye tell hou thocht wes caa'd agley
tae smoor a masterpiece athoot remeid,
fowk nidge an keek an say: *We ken, we ken.*

Donny O'Rourke

LOAM

Steadily my uncle forks an acre
Of suppurating North Antrim top soil
To rich black loam, his shirt a spinnaker
In the snell Nor' Easter. Storm ditches boil
With three days rain, yet shaws ornate as boas
Festoon each year, the shoulder of this hill.
(Sure Planter's lore's a match for Noah's
In things Deluvian). In each ruled drill
Mauve tubers stud the sore disputed ground,
Cold clinging clay soon loosened from the crop;
Soil I shake off less easily bound
In bone to each mulchy friable drop
Of turfy Irish earth. Close packed and wet
That loam's in my brown eyes and fertile yet.

PARALLELS: FOR PC STEPHEN O'ROURKE

In the temporary mortuary
at the ice rink, you spent Christmas Day
body bagging those the pathologist's knife
had gourded. You'd asked us round and Life

Goes On . . . I carved the turkey in your absence
shirking comparisons. Dorothy was tense
the children muted — the crackers they pulled
imploding like a Boeing's pressurised hull

in the dead air space over Lockerbie.
While we scoured the floor for the debris
of a shattered toy, your colleagues searched
the Galloway Hills for bomb fragments. Perched

on the edge of your empty seat we passed the day
resisting the emblems of Tragedy:
in cinnamon scented candles and kitchen smells;
the reek of putrefaction — parallels.

THE ROOMING HOUSES OF AMERICA

I'm the Stranger
the locals call Himself
holidaying wryly
off season in Donegal
sporting tweeds
reading detective novels
being found fascinating.

I'm the Poet
with hair en brosse
idling over pastries
in the Cafe Sperl
gossiping about the Opera
considering an intrigue
with a Frau in furs.

I'm the Drifter
in loose bruised jeans
riding blue rails
stealing guitar licks
from the widows of jazzmen
my only luggage
a pre war Remington

for the novels I tap out drunk
in the rooming houses of America.

Richard Price

RESERVOIR

The river hasn't a legend to stand on —
if the trout could walk on water
they'd see the sea and long for it,
but there are no miracles
on a Council loch, BY ORDER.

It's a haw no a hazel
drappin its boz,
and fur wee manky fish.

No foolish maiden badly praying,
no bingo a Shannon —
your colonial Waverley
cuts no Congo;
Renfrewshire is neither heart nor darkness.

There is the sound of water only.

AQUAFLORA

Specks of cream surface —
the river curdling.
A rope-swing touches water,
bridge crotches go under,
second cars (on credit)
are tided over,
antirrhinums become aquaflora.

At a sill a cup.
A fly like a crippled raven
randomises on the double glazing.
An Easter cactus — June explosions.
The water-line, a hem of air
(a simple ocean),
rises.

DIJON, JUNE 1988

In the hostel, German voices
break the curfew, laughter
and English pop songs
(the Dusseldorf girls)
make it to our empty dorm.
Outside, a showcase
shuffles three adverts.
I miss your shoulders, your French.

'Orangina, ça me pulpes!'
'Café Frappe'. 'Split Spats' —
to visit another country
is to question all advertisements —
with the French I've grabbed
I know I miss the idiom:
my dictionary takes me literally;
lingually, I'm out of pocket.

Is it today's election bills
that make me think of home
(that vague home in nationality) —
the reliable monarchic faces?
Our Prime Minister is awake,
losing sleep for her people,
talking shop in camera;
editing our Bible.

In these suspicious hours
mosquitos materialise on the asleep,
mineral water bought late
works warm,
village-long coal trains
clatter past our wilted flags,
grey-yellow but pan-European
in the grey-yellow light.

Tomorrow, in others' cabriolet sun,
we'll blether our rucksacks to the station,
new Germans will understand
our apologised limitations:
we know no second language
(for the sake of better treatment
we wear the lion rampant.
We mention Glasgow:

it is a useful city, and very famous).

ANIMUS AND *GELB-ROT-BLAU*
After Kandinsky's painting

There were other tricks to the print:
a skinhead on the vertical
a kid's cat inverted —
the tape-worm, black in meander,
got the gut.

All of the times is *Gelb-rot-blau*
the present still: a gift of margarine
and blue-fish, aubergine;
freed dark parfum;
the lines of a radiating box.

Where do I stand for you?
Between your print (a leaving
present) and the counterpane?
I wish for 'art', 'happiness' —
I generalise again.

DECCAN TO ELECTRON

The encyclopaedia: *Collier's* universal quin-
tessence analogue electroencephalogram. A
to ZWORYKIN with Bibliography and Funk and
Wagnall's *International Dictionary* (An-
atomy and Engine guts transparencies)
honestly American: no Chicago *Britannica.*

But inside DECCAN to ELECTRON repeated
COLONNA to DECATUR, Denmark and Dunnet Head
were distant as Edinburgh and Ecuador, Di-
Maggio supped Dover's powder with De Quincey
in the expressible Ether, Dionysius and
Disraeli, one nation, chuckled with De-
mocritus, Dürer kept his landscapes as
Gunn's *Other*; as ever, the Democrats
couldn't speak plain.

There was never a time to know Ecclesiastes
or refrain or not from kenning Einstein like-
wise digested; the Eisteddfid and Druids,
as if spelt from a Devanagari, were mystic
as Detroit autos for no satisfied enquiry.

I wondered lonely as the Diaspora, diamond-
backs, Dobermans, and douroucouli, all
unnamed, hissed, barked, and skreighed —
demi-vierge for being known by others free
(I the obvious cuckold with no droit
de seigneur — such a mother — a Delphic
reject, Dementia praecox in the only-
imagined DNA).

To know Renoir's bathers and not the ballet
of Degas! Drummond, Duns Scotus, and Dunbar
were as the Delaware — extinct but somehow
echoing (if differently) like Doppler (there
is that reverberating hope; electrons now
aren't fundamental).

J.N. Reilly

ST VALENTINE'S DAY

A strange noise. Click, click, click, click, interminably, click click, click.

Somebody at the door.

David dragged himself from bed, prised open his eyes and pulled on his wife's dressing gown. Half asleep and bleary-eyed he stumbled out of the bedroom and along the hallway.

Is that you, Jean? came a woman's voice through the door.

No, it's me, said David, turning the key and opening the door.

Standing before him was Tina Watson, his friend Ricky's mother, all morning fresh and perfumed, a well made woman in her late forties, sparkling with energy, bright eyes, all go and ready for work.

Is Ricky with you, David, she asked urgently.

No. He's eh ... yes ... I think he's over at Sam's, David stuttered, struggling from sleep.

I was wanting to make sure he got back home, said Tina. He's getting a visit from the Social Security this morning.

Yes, he's at Sam's, David yawned. Sam will more than likely wake him up.

Oh well, I'm sorry I got you out of bed, said Tina apologetically.

I was about to get up anyway, he lied.

I'll have to get off to work now. Cheerio.

Cheerio.

She turned and hurried off down the stairs, her perfume lingering with a promise of spring. David closed the door, went back into the bedroom and climbed into bed. Jean lay beside him, fast asleep, soft and soothing with morning smells. He lay for a few minutes drifting back to sleep, but shook himself and made a point of rising. If not, he would have slept until well past noon. He picked up his clothes and went into the living-room, pushed the plugs into their sockets and switched on the electric fire. He sat down on the carpet and

stared somnambulistically at the synthetic coal effect of the
fire and far beyond. He dressed slowly.

He heard a noise at the door. Probably the postman, he
thought distractedly, but could not be bothered going to see
if there was any mail.

On some obscure impulse he decided to go into the bedroom, the legerdemain of sleep still clinging to his brain like
chewing gum.

Jean was out of bed and standing by the dressing table.
He thought he saw a piece of paper in her hand. He gazed
sleepily around the room then asked her what she was doing.

Nothing, she replied innocently, turning towards him.

David shook his head, returned to the living-room and
took his place on the carpet before the fire. Dawn razor,
dawn razor. The words seemed to slice through his brain.
Strange phrases like that had a habit of occurring to him now
and then. They passed as a bus would pass or the seasons
pass, inevitably. He did not wonder whether or not they
possessed meaning. For David their significance lay in the
fact that they arose, he heard them, and then were gone. The
reason that he heard unusual phrases or combinations of
words he put down to having far too much time on his hands,
now that he was unemployed. It stands to reason, he had said
to himself, that when a brain is not occupied with a job of
work then it has to occupy itself.

He could now hear Jean in the kitchen. The rattle of cut-
lery, and the snap of cupboards. She entered the living-room
carrying a bowl of krispies, sat down on the seat by the fire
and began munching away, glowering illhumouredly at him.

David rose, annoyed by her sullenness and said angrily:
I'm away to piss.

A large white envelope lay at the door. He walked past it
and went into the bathroom. He picked it up on his return.
At first he thought that someone had sent a Valentine to
Jean, well it was the fourteenth of February, but it was
addressed to him.

He threw the envelope down in front of the fire. Jean ate
her krispies in silence, still glowering. Eventually he picked
up the envelope and surveyed the handwriting. It did look
familiar. He was embarrassed. Who would want to send a
Valentine to him?

It's from you Jean, isn't it, he said. There's no stamp on
the envelope. It is from you.

From me, she exclaimed. You must be joking. I don't

write as neatly as that.

He ripped open the envelope and took out a large pink card, in the centre of which was an oval photograph of a black and white shaggy dog. Printed inside the card in block capitals were the words: May the sun always shine. He smiled. He definitely knew now. His suspicions were right. It was from Jean. Only she would have written something so ingenuous but fitting.

Thanks Jean. That's nice, really lovely.

He did not know what to say to show how happy he really was. Indeed he had always found difficulty in expressing himself, especially concerning anything affectionate or intimate.

You know I love the sun. No one else could have written that except you.

He went over and switched on the radio.

Do you want a cup of tea? he asked.

Yes, she replied curtly.

What is the matter with her. He could not abide her moods with their attendant accusatory implications. They completely unhinged him, confused him. What had he done wrong he would ask himself. And asking himself that very question, to which he could find no answer, he went into the kitchen and switched on the kettle. A stainless steel D.J. voice seeped in from the living-room, cutting into the furniture, the walls, the pots and pans, the very medulla. He knew it was a bad habit switching the radio on every morning. He would have to make a point not to.

He handed Jean her tea and took his usual place by the fire.

What was that? he shouted furiously, turning and punching sharply against her leg. He was not going to take any more of her snide remarks. Strangely enough he could not remember what she had said. The words she had mumbled maliciously had raced out of his head as fast as they had entered.

Jean jumped up and ran into the bedroom. David chased after her. What can only be described as an ambiguous indignance permeated him.

You're like all the rest. You're no different, Jean screamed.

David ran at her and grabbed her by the throat. Dark strangers rushing through his head, his heart beating madly against his chest, his whole body shaking, he slapped her.

What do you mean, like all the rest? he shouted.

Yeah, you were right last night when you said you weren't into violence, she spluttered. You only like hitting women.

You're right, you're right, he bawled sarcastically.

They struggled and fell onto the bed.

You're right, I'm not into violence.

He held he throat tightly and with his free hand slapped her again. I'm into killing . . . you. You bastard.

He squeezed her throat. But no. His head flashed clear. He leapt away from her and stood by the window: evening paper wife beater and child beater headlines in fresh ink appearing before his eyes.

You're not a man, she screamed. You're a mouse.

He laughed at the banality of her accusations.

I'm not a man, he exclaimed. What in the name of Christ is a man? Show me a man, he shouted, waving his arms frantically in the air.

You're a mouse, she goaded.

He slapped her, suddenly thinking of a boxer he had seen in a magazine his father had shown him when he was a little boy.

Yeah, I'm a fuckin' mouse, he snarled.

Their voices thick with insults drifted into stone-faced silence and memories of drunken Glasgow Friday night children crying, fathers shouting, windows smashed and distant songs.

David turned and went into the living-room. Jean followed.

It's got to stop, Jean.

He lit two cigarettes and handed one to her. Jean sat staring stubbornly into the fire. One of the bars was broken, it lay on its belly and buzzed incessantly. It would not be long before the other bar snapped and the fire would be useless. They could not afford to buy new bars for it.

If you want a divorce, say so, said David. I mean, I don't, but if you do.

The radio spat out malignant teen idop pop charts and the ingratiating sound of electric guitars.

Well what do you want, Jean? he asked again.

There was no reply.

Why can't I keep my babbling mouth shut, he said inwardly, but was compelled to carry through what he had begun. Circumspection was not an attribute of this ordinary young man; if indeed there are such phenomena as ordinary people. He was completely and utterly at the command of his emotions. Now that he was without the regulatory routine of work, he was emotionally stretched to breaking point when with anguish he thought of the bills that had to be paid, that there would be no future if Jean and he could not find some kind of employment.

He continued placidly, wearily, It wouldn't cost anything to get a divorce. Being on Social Security we'd get legal aid. You could get it on the grounds that I'm cruel. I don't mind.

Jean did not say anything. She was still looking at the fire, but sadly now, reminiscing on the old days, before they were unemployed, when they were courting, crossing over that first year of married bliss when everything was perfect. They had gone to discos and danced the night away. Their only concern had been at what type of restaurant they would dine; Chinese, Indian or European. Now she could hardly afford to buy herself a pair of tights, and when she did she bought the cheapest.

I don't know, she heard David intoning guiltily. I just don't know. I'm not violent. Okay, okay, I know that sounds stupid. I'm contradicting myself, what I did. I'm sorry. You know what I mean. Oh what's happening to us? Talk to me, Jean, please.

You hit me, Jean began wistfully. At times like this, when we don't have much, we should pull together, show how much we love each other, 'cause things aren't going to change. I don't see you getting a job. And I know it's not your fault. No, wait a wee minute, I've only got to say that I think at times like this people's true feelings come out, their real character.

But I'm human after all, said David despairingly. I'm human. What am I to do when you say horrible things to me?

You shouldn't have hit me, Jean rejoined. There's never any need, and you've done it before.

I know, said David closing his eyes and shaking his head from side to side in despair. Christ knows I'm sorry. I'm sorry. I really am. But I couldn't help it. I've got a breaking point. Everybody's got a breaking point. Your bad tempered moods drive me crazy. I've watched you for days, sitting doing nothing, your face dour, hardly two words coming from you. And I try to be pleasant. I want to please you. And isn't it true that when you do speak you insult me, you say something rotten?

Still gazing at the fire, Jean nodded her head slowly in

agreement, and then in a pained whisper she said, But you hit me.

I'm sorry, said David pathetically though honestly, and even more pathetically he added, I'll never do it again. Never. I promise.

For what seemed for ever they sat staring into the fire, nothing between them but the buzzing from the fire's broken bar and the intermittent sounds of passing traffic on the street below, until David suggested they should go for a drink.

What do you say? he said. Let's get out of here. A drink would do us the world of good. We need to talk. We need to straighten things out.

You know we can't afford to spend money on drink, Jean remarked, though without reproach.

A drink each won't kill us. Just this once, eh? David implored.

Okay, just this once. Let me get dressed.

While Jean went to the bedroom to dress, David stood at the living-room window, completely desolate, watching the odd car or taxi slide through the hushed drizzle that was falling.

When Jean returned, already wearing her jacket, she was gently touching a slight swelling under her right eye. David felt she was doing that to remind him of his violence and, in so doing, exact punishment knowing that the memory would engender the pain of guilt and remorse.

I'll away and get my jacket, said David.

We'll use my umbrella, Jean called after him. If we take yours it'll probably fall to pieces.

Soon they were out in the rain, sheltering beneath Jean's umbrella and shivering in the cold. Their jackets were of a thin synthetic material and no match for even a temperate winter's day. They would have liked to have had coats, but supplementary benefit does not run to such luxuries.

Oh for ... What's going on, said David, disappointed to find that the door to the pub's lounge would not open.

Without a word, Jean turned and walked away, back towards their flat.

Wait a minute, Jean, David called to her, the bar's open. Just a wee minute. I'll find out why the lounge is closed.

Stepping into the dim smoky yellow light of the bar, David's attention was instantly arrested by the rows of bottles coruscating from the gantry; numerous brands of whiskey, and vodka, bacardi, rum, martini and foreign lagers he had never seen or heard of. He went over to the counter and tried to attract the attention of the barmaid, while on a shelf to the right of the dartboard, a colour television flickered a raddled middle-aged woman whispering cookery hints of onion and sauce into the worn retired ears and faces of the old men, and the pale young men of dole queues desolate, playing dominoes with hushed voices and intermittent laughter which was strained and too loud.

The barmaid joked with the few customers standing at the counter and poured drinks, seemingly ignoring David's gestures to attract her attention.

Excuse me, he called out eventually. Doesn't the lounge open any more during the afternoon?

It's closed, the barmaid replied so curtly that David began to feel he had asked something terribly stupid.

Yes, I know, but . . .

It's closed, the barmaid snapped again and turned away to serve someone, leaving David gazing at her coquettish wiggle as she went to the other end of the counter. He made to leave. The blue bloused cookery woman on the television pursed her lips and whispered of garlic. David felt someone tap his shoulder. It was the old guy he had seen standing at the bar. Coughing, the old guy explained, The lounge is only on part-time now, son. They don't open it in the afternoon anymore. Only at night.

The old guy took a sip of whiskey and his cough worsened.

Thanks, I didn't know that. It's been a good long while since I was last here.

That's right, son, they only open the lounge at night.

Well, thanks again for telling me.

David left a fit of coughing clawing at the old guy's chest and throat, and he hurriedly left the bar when he saw a young man opening his jacket to reveal a large carving knife to the man standing drinking beside him.

A faint smile passed over Jean's lips. She looked more alive and fresh now. More like the girl David used to know. Her imperviousness was passing.

Why wasn't it open? she asked him.

They only open at night now. They're on part-time, he replied. Let's forget about booze and get some coke and crisps or something from the newsagent's? What do you say?

Yes. Come on, said Jean, and then we'll go home and snuggle up in front of the fire and watch the afternoon movie.

Alan Riach

AT LOUDOUN HILL

At Loudoun Hill
in its sleep
on the Strathaven Road
on the dreamy edge of Ayrshire
and Lanarkshire,
                in one of the many
corners of this folding map,
where incidental blood once streaked the grass,
and I can't remember now what time
of day it was or even
if I read what time of year —
    It would be cold, like this,
sunlight like teeth, and the yellow grease
on swords and harnesses; even now —
that horse over there: its teeth
have the colour of the day,
and its sound —
                By Loudoun Hill, now,
between Arran and Strathaven,
between the submarines and the frigates
and the gardeners and the forget-me-nots
and the profiteers and the ignorant;
between Arran and the leafy burghs of small-town
Scotland, half-awake, if only that,
where (my Grandfather told me) the only
excitement seen in the streets
was the fairly regular visit of
the hearse . . .
                By Loudoun Hill, its odd isolate
                shoulder-shape
                in the Farmers' fields
                in Lanarkshire, in
                the Common Market.

I was driving back,
from Arran, and
the sight of it passing
my shoulder made me think a
little about the trip, and I
couldn't imagine I had
made it alone. What does it mean
to be so modern
                              at Loudoun Hill?
with the smell of cow
dung and horsebacks,
the sheep's wool toughness in the grass,
the blotched cows in their loneliness,
the colours in the landscape mainly easy, mostly
tonally the same: redundant greys,
redundant greens. Only
the shoulder
of the hill goes into the wind, goes
                              into the mind
like another thing,
                    like you
pass through a door
and it's another place, there is something 'still strong
still unflinching in spirit.'

So I stopped the car
and I stood there with a gaunt eye, but not, now,
watching the armies of men on the hillside
and the men on the level fields
preparing their senses and their long blades getting
keener,
but looking at a recent incremental recognition
of who was never there, but holds it
all in balance, now, at Loudoun Hill,
                              money-eyed,
watching.

AT WORK

When you cannot clean it out at all,
When you can not clean it out
easily, or
        at all —
your broken nails, the
smell and texture of the oil,
the grit of stones from out
such depths you reach
and mark each day:
       3260′ to 6110′
your knuckles' skin scraped off on
       wooden ammunition boxes,
full of wet sacks,
            your breath
clogged by the dust risen
from the cartons of small
washed and dried stone
cuttings: say, from
       22/16a-2z (North
Sea) (Some rigs
already being off
the west coast,
and new lines
of transport being planned for,
through Oban, for example, we
must be at another turn
or else have taken it)
      or, say: Box 2 Set E, samples
taken from 2800′ to 9210′
at 10′ intervals (Set E might
run from Box 1 to Box 31)
— Noting such information
like vertical shafts in the brain,
polyhedrons of the possible across
a whole economy's domain:
Then shelving these same
runs of information
with the fork-lift trucks,
lifting such
as those ammo boxes (marked:
MOD, explosives! but full

of those wet sacks, those
samples) or those other
            big white plastic boxes
            (4$'$ x 2$'$ x 1½$'$)
            of washed and dried cuttings
            732 of them. (I
            counted and numbered them. That
            was part of it too.) They
            filled 2 rows of shelving
            up to 20 times a man's height:
            it made that part
            of the warehouse look
            like a mortuary for midgets.
And then as well those
wooden trays
on which, slices of core samples
were frozen on resin
and laid out in order;
and then the long square wooden boxes,
6$'$ x 4$''$ x 4$''$
for the scals, the preserved samples,
straight out of the depths, lumps
of uncut deadweight
from all those drillholes
into the earth.
            Trays of plugs
            Boxes of trays
            Crates of boxes
            Boxes of cartons
            Boxes of boxes
            Shelves of boxes
            Rows of shelves
            Bays of rows (as high as 20 men)
            And a warehouseful of shelves of bays, that slid
            Along flush with each other (to save
            Space) at the touch of a button. And between
            The bays, just space to turn
            A forklift truck, deftly.
            And around the warehouse,
off at the sides, rooms
of tables and instruments, for
looking, and chemicals, for
testing, these samples, for
oil.

And it didn't clean out
easily,
the smell and texture
          and the taste.
I took
6 months of it
but they found me reading a book in the teabreak.
My contract came to an end.

A SHORT INTRODUCTION TO MY UNCLE GLEN

Glen was always building sheds. He'd buy
wood. He had a thing about building sheds. He built
six stables in his garden, then realised
he'd have to buy the horses for them (and did). He built
     at least
three aviaries and more kennels than I can remember.
He filled the aviaries with parrots and canaries
from Australia, Pacific Islands. He always
had dogs: alsatians, a great dane he would dance with
around the kitchen, before he was married. Now,
his kitchen cupboards are full of his kids' litters of jack
     russells.
He used to like Lonnie Donegan.
He used to play the guitar and yodel like Frank Ifield.
At every piece of news to-day you tell him
he looks amazed and shakes his head and says: 'My, my!'
A couple of years ago some of the family took a week's
holiday in Tenerife. Glen was walking on the beach
with my father, talking. Apart from the army,
when he'd been in England and learned to be a chef
(and cook these great sweet yellow curries)
he had never been out of Scotland much. He said
to my father, 'Jimmie,' (which is his name) 'you've
sailed about the world a few times.' (Which is true.)
'Tell me,' he said,
'Where exactly are we?'
Surely,
it's the best way to travel.

THE MIDDLE PASSAGE

one's native land is never fixed and anchored in place; in this age and time, it is always *crumbling*: 'crumbling within a capacity of vision which rediscovers the process to be not foul and destructive but actually the constitutive secret of all creation wherever one happens to be.'

                                                    Wilson Harris

it's dark as the sky outside
the plane I'm sitting in, diametered against,
through earth, the opposite sun,
and pursuing it more slowly. Dawn
will creep up on me, slip over
my shoulder — but this long night,
heading west, like a fool,
like a young man, slowly

the text that bears us on
a heavily freighted airline no
more conscious of ourselves
our numberless ineptitudes
and what unnerving logic
keeps us capsuled in its implicated pieces
running to its terminal moraine: a backyard,
brickdust, humus, essays in permanence
continuous, inviting ivy, requiring
myths and slogans, workable muttered oaths,
shouts in the street, programmes and plans,
reanimate debris, people

beyond all that is henceforth/backthere, this,
at the lowest estimate, rubble, stone, a
halfbrick (it goes further than
a whole one when you throw it)
pick it up why not why don't you?

THE URGENCY

A man has been burned. What I remember only is the
    aftermath,
with the ambulance and male nurses outside the ruined and
smouldering building. They're lifting a man on a stretcher
but a winecoloured blanket is wrapped all round his body;
    only
his head is visible. And it is a naked skull, its eyesockets
empty, all bone and teeth, no skin or flesh, no blood, just
bone. But the jaw and teeth are moving: he is talking, and
    his
words go on and on and they are very loud in my head. I
    can
understand nothing he says. Only his words are loud. He is
turning his skull around, facing one bystanding nurse and
    then
another, without sensitivity, without flesh. One man bends
down and lifts the corner of the blanket and places it over his
head. Not feeling it, being nerveless, fleshless, sightless, he
goes on talking, and goes on talking. We cannot see him now
beneath the blanket.

Iain Robertson Scott

THE HELMET

Now it is impossible to see through the visor because of the
blood. It is as if someone had dipped a broad brush into a can
of wine-dark paint and then drawn it across the perspex.

It is my blood. I touch it. I discover that it is not smooth,
but gently-grained — just like a smear of oils. I rub the edge of
the visor to discover if the colour is fixed hard, but a tiny
fragment flakes off on my thumb. I stop, not to spoil any
more.

When I revived from the coma, it was the first thing I remembered. But perhaps that is not true. I asked my parents, sitting
by the white hospital bed, what had happened to my bike
and helmet? My father said that the bike had been totally
wrecked, but was still in the possession of the police — so was
the helmet. It all amounted to 'evidence', he said. I could, I
can, remember very little. My father spoke softly, as though
I would never have to see these objects again — he supposed
this would be reassuring. I insisted that the helmet should be
kept: they must save it for me. My mother tried to calm me
by taking my hand and agreeing to my wish, in a voice normally reserved for baby-talk. I knew she would betray me.

As the weeks passed in the white, chromium ward, I continued to demand a promise that the helmet would not be
thrown away. Finally they acceded. Probably some doctor
had advised them that any further denial might upset my re-
covery. My mother was clearly distressed, but she affected a
compromise: 'Very well, I'll clean it up and see what can be
done to repair it ... get it back to its original condition.'

'Always the tidy little housewife,' I thought. She had to
find a way of domesticating my beast.

I dreamed of us arguing, the usual low, restrained argument, which seemed to throb and hum, until my mother
would say: 'I only want things back as they were.'

'Well I don't' I muttered, probably aloud, because then
I woke. My parents looked at me as though I had screamed.

Everyone was so nervous of me then, so alarmed.

But I needed that helmet untouched.

It was there on the bottom shelf of my wardrobe when I returned home from hospital. Next to the newly polished shoes and boots, sitting in the darkness of the jackets and coats. I lifted it out and held it before me as though I were about to crown myself. I placed it on the pink candlewick bedcover and sat beside it.

The only dent on the shiny, black shell was at the front where the paint had flaked off to reveal the metal skull beneath. I tried to lift up the visor but it held fast, blind-red. I examined the inside to discover the problem. The screws were unharmed but caked dry-hard, and immoveable with blood. I pressed the back of my hand down into the foamy black padding of the cranium. It cupped my hand in warmth. I held it there for several minutes.

I replaced the helmet in the wardrobe and rarely mentioned it again. I had discovered that it merely worried people — its continued presence seemed to demonstrate that I was still far from well. Not quite back to normal. I found the subject of my accident rather interesting, however, and I used to enjoy terrifying relatives by describing it in ghoulish detail. I have always had a black sense of humour. Only my two small cousins relished the story with the same amount of glee as myself. I retold it to them so often — like a Grimm's fairy tale.

It had been a head-on collision. The other driver had allowed his car to wander over on to the wrong side of the road. He was not even drunk, just day-dreaming on a warm summer's afternoon, yellow fields of rape as far as the foot-hills. I remember that still — then trying to brake, or turn, or just get me out of here. That was ten months ago.

The result was broken arms and legs and head injuries. I still walk slowly with the aid of a stick. I shall never have that 'manual dexterity' which I had before. What they mean is that I shall never be able to draw or paint in a style any more sophisticated than a child's. My hand is now too weak. Even my writing trails off the line down the page. When I was a boy I sometimes signed off letters like that, pretending I was dying — life slipping away.

'You will need to retrain, now that teaching is out,' the psychologist said. 'I would suggest a desk job in an office. Possibly computers. Computer graphics. Same sort of line as

before, different medium. Have you used computers? ...
I think you might find the whole experience quite exciting. It
doesn't need to be regarded in a negative light at all. Imagine
it as an opportunity to start again. Just at the time, in your
early thirties, when most men feel that things are becoming
too settled and humdrum anyway.'

I suppose he was only trying to be encouraging — everyone is so relentlessly positive and cheerful. Nobody merely
listens and agrees. Every doubt I express has to be countered
and squashed, never admitted. And so accidents and illnesses
are translated into unsuspected boons. Never have I been
deemed so lucky, so often. 'You're lucky to have your sight
— your mind — your limbs — you're lucky you weren't killed,
or worse.'

Motorbikes have attracted me since I was twelve years old.
On Saturday afternoons I would stand in front of Stein's, the
cycle shop, wondering at the machines. Machines of low,
sleek chromium and power. It was their beauty which always
attracted me. I hardly rode my bike in winter because of
the mud and rain. I did not like it to become ugly with dirt.
When I did venture out, I would return to sponge it down
carefully in my father's garage.

Then there was the speed. I do admit to that. But I was a
careful driver; it was only on those lonely stretches of High-
land road which I knew so well that I would really let go. Of
course, when I was seventeen, I used to rev up the engine,
waiting at traffic lights, and roar along city streets — but that
was just typical of my age. I have never been interested in
riding with others, in a pack. I rode a bike to be alone. To be
the hard, black shell, powering along the road: hills and for-
ests all around, and no one but me to think about. Not even
that, beacuse I do not remember ever thinking in any rational
way. Just sensation without mind. The corners were always
best: I think I enjoyed speed just for the sensation of corner-
ing. The seat dips until it almost touches the tarmac of the
road. One hundred miles an hour and safer than many motorists at forty, because I am in balance with the machine, acting
and reacting as one, indivisible, object. The wind smacking
and passing through my body.

My favourite route was to leave Edinburgh and cross the
Forth Road Bridge to Fife: the low, rich farming land; hedge-
rowed, cubist squares of yellow corn and green. The stone
towers and red pan-tiled roofs of country houses, just visible

over a curtain wall of thick trees. Then northwards, past
Dunkeld, sometimes as far north as Braemar and Ballater —
and back — all in one day. That final stretch was best of all,
climbing the steep road that scorches into the barren back of
Glen Shee. Rock and scree and bald stone hill-sides all around
at the summit, but then the free-wheeling decline, undulating
along the roads that fall down to Braemar. The land becoming
greener, more wooded, the hills becoming gentler. I would
stop and eat my lunch by the side of a burn or high up on a
ridge overlooking the glen. At first all seemed silent and solit-
ary, but as my ears became attuned — sounds of wings and
winds and the click of undergrowth. I still felt alone, but
more peaceful. A sense, temporarily lost, now returned. I
could never understand why motorists were satisfied to eat
their meals on plastic chairs, in a lay-by. Or why some of my
friends would roar up to country pubs and drown the afternoon in beer.

I had no wish to see my bike after the accident — all that
was left of it.

I remember all of this much more clearly than the events of
last week or yesterday. I remember it all as if I were in it
now, dipped into it, and in this warm liquid, it is always
bright. The dull days (and surely they must have been the
majority?) have been erased completely. All that is left is
feeling and heat.

My head injuries were not too severe, but serious enough
to affect my ability to remember even the most obvious facts.
Just as the accident scratched itself from my memory, so it
clawed away most of the recent past; even the last eight
months, since I left hospital, are difficult to recall. The surgeon explained that, during the accdient, my head had suffered
a severe pounding. Thanks to my helmet the skull had not
been crushed or fractured, but the brain inside, which rested
in some sort of plasma, had been buffeted from side to side.
In the process it had swollen and pressed on nerves which
governed the memory. He said that it would take two years
for the brain to settle and, only then, would they know how
much of my memory had returned. So I wait passively to discover how much of me is recoverable from a past which I
have largely forgotten.

But it is that previous, forgotten state which everyone
else remembers first, when they meet me. Because of my illness, no one will be deliberately unkind to me ever again:

from now on I am condemned to bring out the best in people and, increasingly, I learn to reflect their goodness. I seem to have attained a state of grace through accident and loss. I cannot be my old self ever again in any way, physically or mentally. I am now the illness and life continues more essentially, as in a city without electricity.

That is why the helmet is so important. Wrapped in the darkness of a cupboard for the rest of my life, it can be my never-changing self-portrait. The artist at thirty. Sometimes, when there is no one at home, I sit and stare at the red visor and imagine that dimly, through its opacity, something stirs beneath, and then I lift it up and slip it over my head. But I can see nothing, I only feel the soft, warm redness. I flop back into the comfort of the bed and curl up, contented.

'Why do you keep that rather gruesome object?' the doctor asked.

'Because of it, I am here.'

Jenny Turner

LORRAINE

This woman, thirtyish, with stringy blonde hair (dyed first yellow then later streaked with ash, it seems to me) is sitting cross legged on the settee in a tight but smarty fawn suit. She is getting on at me, seated on the floor, for being ridiculous; she is doing a monologue, or so it seems to me, passive impassive and utterly polite, sitting just sitting there down on the floor. She goes on and on and on and on and I sit there nodding and making little sympathetic and agreeing noises. I agree I am ridiculous. I agree I am ridiculous. Because this would make no sense at all you can see I am really thinking of something quite different.

I have got at least one eye set to the shortbread sat on a plate over by the fire. I've got my mouth crammed full of jacket crisps, and my hands round tea all sloshed in the saucer. I'm wishing there was something a bit softer to ogle at, some egg and tomato finger rolls maybe. Something with some give for my poor cracked gums. Or less heavily salted, would be a start. You have to just go for it, this woman is declaiming, you have to get up and go. Get to a certain age and it all just flounders past. Take it from me. Take it from granny. She is talking so loud, all the other girls laugh at this point. I know. I can tell. She's got the whole room for an audience and she's aiming it at me. She is saying how ridiculous she finds me, and all I can do is look up past her knees with big blue eyes, secretly involved in the stuffing of my face.

I am thinking that maybe there are sexual over or undertones to this conversation, that maybe this woman fancies me rotten but has no way to admit or express it. Why should she, she has a small mean ring on her engagement finger, she is Head of the Business Studies department in some school and teaches not just typing but also Accounts. Or maybe me her. By agreeing to be found ridiculous maybe I am consenting to be being all walked over, being all walked over being, a way of wondering about the inconceivable sexual act. Ridiculous! It is more than barely possible that a conversation held in

someone or other's fussy front room carries no such dimen-
sion at all. Beyond slight amusement at this woman's un-
knowing, and the ridiculousness of her sitting there telling me
I am ridiculous I couldn't really tell you what I make of it at
all. The crux so far is her sitting there telling me I'm ridiculous.
The question is how to get at the biscuits with the semblance
of politeness left unrent.

Her crossed legs are like lard below the knee, melted and
hardened, clad in that shade of fifteen denier that used to get
called Ecru. Meaning the colour of unbleached linen which,
no matter that you dash away will not sit right, it cannot
take a crease, so there is one possibility for a joke. Whatever,
the fawn skirt from my vantage point is wrinkled tight over
the pelvis, the safari look top to match bags over the hard
belted fat waist. With tedium I note a loose thread stuck to
one of the shoulder pads, that she spits a bit when speaking.
Black makeup gunk, and maybe a bit of broken lash, begin to
gather and clog at one corner of an eye.

Being a schoolteacher she must have strategies, methods
for dealing with underarm sweat, in folds round the loins,
under eyes, wherever. The hot eyes causing black to collect in
tiny lines, streaked dark in any case, through lack of enough
sleeping, through overwork and going out weekday nights.
She was speaking earlier, about once meeting a bunch of her
fourth year tinks on a Wednesday night, Mr Trontis dance-
hall: randy on a shandy. Randy for a shandy. Gordon was sic
affronted, she said, he just stuck his head behind my arm and
wouldn't come out all night. It's not as if it's usually an
under agers' spot. You have to dress smart. There's not usually
casuals and schemies. No trainers, no jeans, no colours.

My brain is well softened by the continuous ingestion of
carbohydrate and weak tea, and I am wanting to ask how
teachers consider the feasibility of personal plumbing systems
up the lift and separate of their foundation garments, the
better to organise pheromone-free disposal of the pedagogical
sweat. You must have to be chary, as a teacher, what you do
with your sweat. The 'kids' can be, almost human really, run
into somewhere, for a night out on the ran dan, but in a
classful of themselves fairly well sweated out adolescents,
ADOLESCENTS if you see, er sweat calling sweat and crikey.
What like of good places are there to go then, my pulled out
choke pipes up. Is there somewhere nice for a weekday night.

Now you're ASKING, heh girls, she's asking, she says.
And long drawn out, w-e-l-l l-e-t m-e s-e-e. I puff gnomically

on a cigarette, held in the thumbs and forefingers of both hands. But I don't know heh, that it'd be YOUR cup of tea. You don't suppose this woman is treating me as a child? 'Thirtyish!' If you could only know the dismissal implicit in such a characterisation! That leaking system, those years of early middle age!

And what of me: do I not sweat? It does not seem to be at issue yet, not here, not now. I am unaware of having any. I'm desperately just sitting here, looking just looking, all so self-possessed. Staring into the fire. Stretching over to get an ash tray without my bottom lifting off the floor. Sorry ah me sorry, you were saying to me. I beg your pardon. Bup pardon. Ah ah. Hum. HUM. Sweat in the crux of arms folded, thigh on thigh, in the corners of underwear and elasticated bits and pieces holding in. Lift and separate. Beginning to run through palms clamped one on each hip in a telling-off gest- ure. After class I'm sure the 'kids', the young ones copy it openly, smirking. She was doing it to me as well, though only momentarily, to underline a point, and as a gesture to my ostensibly adult status and to her own suspicion as to its validity or worth, with a blithe touch of the flagrant, of the parody to it.

So maybe then she doesn't mean it, this crap she's saying and goes on saying to me. I should butt in tactfully and change the subject perhaps. I've seen her picture in Gail's album, as bridesmaid at the wedding of another of the teachers from the school. It had a fifties theme and her skirt stuck way out with a strapless bodice, real satin, turquoise, with a darker blue trim. I can admire it. I can show I've got manners. I can ask what has happened to the frock now, what can be done with it after the event. I ask after Gordon. Gordon got a new coat the other day, for going to Canada in, camel coloured and double breasted and cost £179.95. It was in a sale half price. Buy dear, you buy once. Buy dear you buy once. Take it from me. I thought she was doing a music hall impression of somebody. But she's doing it straight. Buy dear you buy once. I cannot decide what I make of her, ridiculous or any other wise, and what that makes me, just sitting here and nodding. I've got at a lump of the shortbread and she's telling me, she doesn't know where I put it all. She has to watch the figure. One day you wake up one morning and too late, you're landed with it. There's nothing you can say to that. No matter that I coax her, draw her out on the subject of this coat, she is making it very clear she finds me lacking. No bones about it.

She's openly attempting to escalate the situation. Drawing others in with fell sweeps of the eye. She can't lean forward, picking at a point in her stories with a Mexican Corn Chip, without looking like she's some vast amphibious animal struggling through a hole. Shoes flat to the ground now, arms out wide, the crux is her arse lodged at the back of the settee, orthopaedically designed to tilt back, with a ridge to hold the knees. Hold what. She is now on the subject of the suit he got to go with it, for Canada, cashmere mix, thin stripe. Buy dear you buy once and so forth. I am smiling up at her, lost in the apparition of my own blue eyes, rolling a ball of chewed biscuit round and round my mouth.

I suddenly know what I'm thinking and it isn't irrelevant or ambivalent at all. I am thinking, ridiculously, that I should like to edge over the shaggy pile and grab this woman by the base of her high heeled white pointy toed shoes. The heel is white also, 'leather' covered in one piece, and stuck into the sole right-angled, exactly like a wrench. If I get it in my fist I can bend it round till either the woman flops over prostrate or the heel comes away in my hand. Realistically it would be the latter that would happen, the shoes are sold as fashion wear only, not at all durable and not designed to be heaved at.

And then how would this woman ever make it home! Wobbling on feet aligned backwards, waving one white heel in her hand at a speeding past taxi and all other subsequently speeding past taxis, shoulder bag thumping into her backside as she pants and swears under her breath and tries to look respectable and fetching. But no in point of fact, this woman would ring Gordon. He'd come fleeing down the carriageway, gas turbo injection, in answer to her very call. As this woman was cultivating Gordon and battering children into submission with her stupidity and girth, waving arms about, buying gear, giving dirty looks and smart remarks I was hard at it supposedly, developing muscles in my body and brain. I should know enough to get myself elegantly out of this one. I learned to be an excellent conversationalist, and have yet to turn this situation to such a point as I can start talking about myself.

Isabella M. Walker

THREE STORIES

I The Song of the Caul 1938

Other than when I sang the song myself I have heard it only twice in my lifetime.

It all started in the 1930s when as a child of four I was nearly drowned in Dowies Mill leid.

She never liked me saying so but I stood outside of myself and watched them lift my body from the river. But then my mother never was one to tolerate anything tinged with the unnatural.

Still, I would insist that I had been able to watch them drag me out from just above the dam-heid — a floating bundle of rags one of the mill-workers had at first thought.

Of the women folk Mrs Murray was first on the scene. I was slippery with oil from the mill workings so she looped up her skirts to cradle me in and ran up to my mother's wash-house.

Someone had alerted Granny Crane, the old woman in black who helped bring folk into the world and saw that they were fittingly dressed to leave it.

Mrs Hopkins must have thought I was dead; she was covering her wee boy's face with her apron.

Granny Crane started tossing me from a zinc bath of stone cold water over into a wooden tub of hot, hot water. She kept at it. Back and forth I went.

My mother was distraught trying to stop her. 'Mary, Mary,' she was crying, 'let me have the bairn.'

Dirty mill-leid water started gurgling up into my throat and down my nose. At last I was able to draw breath and let out a whimpering cry.

'Thair noo,' said Granny Crane, passing me over to my mother, 'nae bairn that comes intae this world wi its caul ower its heid, gangs oot o it through drouning.'

But that was only half the story.

There was the song: and the singing.

II The Herring 1966

They say that herring is the poor man's fish. Well, my father liked his herring — coated in oatmeal.

His parents died when he was yet a boy and he was brought down from Orkney to Leith to be brought up by two Victorian maiden aunts. But in the weathered complexion and the dark eyes always scanning the horizon, I think a part of my father lived on some island yet to surface from the seas.

I was glad that he was buried within sound of the tides with the gulls circling and girning overhead that day.

About a week after his funeral the kindly fish wifie, back from her annual holiday, rapped hastily on my mother's door. 'Fine day. That's yer auld man's herrin.'

My mother took some coins from her peany pocket, paid for the single fish and walked through to the scrubbed wood table that has served a growing family.

She folded back the thin white paper wrapping. Her clenched fist thumped the table-top in grief and rage. An auld man's herring. Raw. Gutted. And coated in oatmeal when it should have shifted with the shoals, a darting streak in the cold northern light.

III   The Kist   1982

Clumsily she clutched me by the sleeve, nudging me across
the room towards the kist at the foot of her bed. When I was
a child she had told me that it had belonged to her mother,
the grandmother I had never known.

'There is something I want you to have,' she said, slurring
the words. I hated how the stroke had left her.

We stood together looking down at the closed lid of this
stout pine Victorian chest. She looked over her shoulder. It
was as if she feared someone might lurk in the shadowy corners of the room witnessing something she wished to be kept
secret.

Somehow, it did not seem right that I should open the
kist, but I knew that she might check her fingers if she
attempted to do so. However, a flourish of her arm indicated
that I should raise the lid. Leaning on its side, she got down
in front of the kist in a kneeling position. For some seconds
she remained motionless and I thought of figures in the atti-
tude of prayer.

Now she set about lifting aside several items wrapped
loosely in brown paper. She paused at a framed photograph
wrapped in newspaper, yellow with age, but then tried on an
elbow-length glove, fumbling with the tiny covered buttons.

'There should be a button-hook somewhere,' she was
muttering. It was as if she had forgotten that I was there. I
suspected that, in her loneliness, she had gone through this
ritual time and time again. Now she opened the shuttle, the
small side compartment, and started to take out something
from amongst crumpled tissue paper. Momentarily, my
eyes were averted. A tiny silver-winged moth, disturbed,
fluttered upwards as if to settle in the curtain folds.

Still kneeling in front of me, my mother looked up.
Loosely across her upturned palms lay a deep purple velvet
sash, the kind a Victorian girl might wear around the waist of
a party dress. In a beautiful clear voice she said, 'Ella, I want
you to keep this. I wore it on the first night that I met your
father.'

A tremor of joy went through me at the way in which the
words were spoken. It was her voice of 'before the stroke'.

I caressed the softness of the velvet, marvelling at how
the sash had kept its depth of tone. 'But you have never

shown me this before,' I ventured.

When I looked down for her response she could not reply. Her body lay slumped against the side of the kist. I did not need to turn her face towards me. I knew that she was dead.

Standing there, it seemed to me as if time stood still. And yet the tick of her antique wall clock still throbbed away. That damned stubborn old clock that only she could coax back into action when it stopped. Strangely, I found myself wondering what would become of it, now that she was dead.

I lifted my mother up onto her bed and attended to her. I then went forward to her mother's kist. Gently, I closed the lid.

I knew that within the hour the outside world and the affairs of death would come rushing in on me but, in the meantime, I was caught up in my own thoughts.

I walked towards the window and glimpsed the moth fluttering through the top opening, out into the uncertain winter sunshine. The late afternoon winter light had always saddened me, reminding me of endings and loneliness, and yet it was a beautiful thing to watch, the winter light.

As I turned to face into her room, I noticed that the light filtering the bare branches of the sycamore tree played a dancing pattern across the white woven bedcover.

It was then that it happened. I heard it again; the song, the song of the caul, the song they could never understand, the song I had heard as a child when drowning.

Bill Watt

THE VALLEY

It was a valley lost in time,
its dinosaurs the machines
that would one day fill it in.
Above it, avuncular hills
were compressed into contours,
not by the slow sift of the years,
but by ranks of grey council houses
where we had been sent, from
smooth-stoned closes, from
square city yards that had been declared
unfit to live in.

                We boys made
the valley our walled garden.
Its slopes lilted with four-leaf
clover, even if we never found any.
Though once we found wild strawberries,
tiny buds of sweetness nestling
in dry grass below a railway line.
Groundnuts too: for the first time
it seemed possible to live
without shops or parents.

But it was hardly paradise:
there was the sudden obscene nest
where on the blue debris of shells
dead fledgelings lay stiff, throttled with wire:
embalmed in their own albumen.
'The Big Boys did that,' a hushed voice said.
Big Boys. Their actions always offstage,
they were the first dark footprints on snow.

I went back there recently,
stood in a field of wilting memories.
The school they built on the valley
had been closed because of falling rolls.
Behind, the skyline of my youth
had become a twisted mouth beneath
massed clouds moving west — a reminder,
while the birds hurtled overhead
like metal shavings from a lathe,
to trust in nothing holding fast.

A GOOD HEAD

Behind him hang fifty pairs of antlers,
strung up on a barbed wire fence
like a necklace of skeletal teeth.
'That one,' he says, 'is an ugly head.'
Indicating two erect branched horns
that rise in parallel symmetry.
'An ugly head. The good heads, the strong,
we leave to . . . beautify the hillside.'
He points out a good head, its antlers
outstretched like a missionary's embrace.
'Had to kill it too, though: it was old.
An act of charity for the beast
and good sport for the paying customer.
It benefits both ways.' He stands there,
arbitrator between nature and pragmatism,
a bent stick of a man in brown cloth,
his eyes shaded by the brim of a brown cap.
On his honed skin there is no hint of stubble.

He has a good head on him too:
runs an efficient estate, lives quotas and tallies.
He can smell the seasons in the heather,
read weather by the shadow on the hills.
His tanned fingers seem designed for the stick,
the gun, the knife, for binoculars.

At the head of the glen, framed by two round hills
as unyielding as iron, squats a bare stone lodge.
Its facade is perfectly rectangular, no frills:
a sentinel for this bare brown landscape
shaved of all unruly life.

WHELKS

A sound like marbles chinking in a bag:
whelks underfoot. My Uncle Dan would eat them
ripe from the beach while we, more wary,
lanced them with safety-pins from well-boiled shells.
All these are empty. Gulls, and other molluscs,
have scooped the flesh and left the husks.

Snotters on pins is how I remember them:
the poor relations of the sea-shore.
And yet — a whorled shell in my hand resembles
helmet and armour of Uccello's St George,
his oxtered lance in the dragon's eye
with the precision of a scalpel. Long ago.

Other kinds of shell are found here too.
Across the Clyde, once rife with men and boats,
a lone oil platform rusts in the dry docks —
an armoured spider on rigid legs.
Upstream the quayside cranes look down
like the last vultures at the last supper.

Rummaging through the slack mosaic beneath
I find a baby whelk — periwinkle really,
a tiny dragon with its tail in its mouth.
And around it the lines of my life, head, heart
have been etched in tributaries of sand.

The waves beat a drumroll on the strand.

MY PARENTS ...

My parents have both been touched by fear.
Once during the war my mother,
unable to thole the blackout,
drew back the curtains and looked out.
Glimpsed rooftops glistened like fish scales
under the cold Clyde moonlight — till
a German plane splintered the stars
and gutted the slates with tracer fire.
As she staggered back, the house rocked
with an infinite unfairness.

Diving from a boat near Carrick
my father met, twenty feet down,
the glowering silence of a basking shark.
In an instant he came face
to face with survival: no point
in any later explanations
of giants that just ate plankton.
For hours he talked in quiet tones
of its gliding mass, carbuncled hide,
the face I thought could have braved all
now strangely humble and confused.

I like to draw the blinds at night
and keep my feet dry in the wet.
Yet at times I envy the sudden
pure simplicity of these fears.

Bill Watt

BRAMBLES

The square notices both signalled the approaching country-side and, with a sting in the tail, pointed to its transience:

PRIVATE

NO DUMPING

TREE FELLING PROHIBITED

FOR FUTURE DEVELOPMENT

She hurried him on, anxious to escape the trough of shadow they were in. The two of them were walking past the last estate on the west of the New Town, only partly visible behind a tarred palisade of planks. (Her father always insisted on the distinction between a council *scheme*, where they lived, and a private *estate*, which was for middle class mortgages.)

The August evening sunlight was good to the New Town: it softened it. The harled buildings had a honeyed depth of colour normally lacking in their hard-edged planes. The bleached grass of the verges, stubbled with little conifers on sticks, glowed green and gold. She wondered idly if she would still be here when all these trees grew tall and the buildings began to look as if they belonged. Not if she could avoid it.

'Where the hell are we supposed to be now?' he said half to himself. 'I've about had it with this game, sweetheart.'

'Near the new roundabout, I think. One of the new roundabouts anyway. Just go on a bit further. I want some space around me. It's oppressive here.'

'Oppressive?' he mimicked. 'You know, you're too smart to be just a frozen pea packer.'

'Pea *grader* if you don't mind. I told you a million times. And it's only a job. It doesn't have to be forever.'

'Aye, you can say that again.'

When she'd first met him, nearly a year ago, he'd been

working on a site. Now he was on a YTS scheme, filling time, growing cynical and hostile.

A blue van roared past. She recognised it as one of the fleet which serviced the estates. Schemes. FRESH VEG DA LY was blazoned in partly-erased capitals on the side. The driver had smiled at her a few times when it was parked in their street. In its wake the van shook up clouds of the pink dust that seemed to coat every gutter in the town. She turned away quickly from the swirls. Black (suede jacket, skirt, tights) was not the most practical colour for walking streets full of builders' spillage. Just as well she had laid off the black lipstick.

'Flash bastard.'

He was on his third can of Special Brew, enough to have made him drunk. Leg-openers he called them, she remembered with a frown. He lurched to the side, then whirled round the pole of a road sign to face her. The dying light made his pale blue eyes almost colourless; on the other hand it flecked his stiff fair hair with red strands.

'Are you too smart for me, do you think?' he asked.

'What's smart? Who cares?'

Her coolness deflated him. She had noticed recently that when he drank too much he became aggressive towards her. It was like he wanted to take the future out on her now.

'So where to now?' he asked, swaying a little.

She shrugged.

'You decide for a change,' he said. 'Instead of just tagging along with me all the time.'

'We could go and pick brambles.'

'That's what I like about you. Never know what to expect next.'

He put his arm around her shoulder and then released her to take another pull at his can. She recoiled a little from his leather jacket. A year ago it had seemed cool; now it looked dirty and smelled sour.

'I mean it. I know where there are some bramble bushes. Not far from here.'

'Catch me at that game.'

'You said I was to decide. I'd like to do it.'

'I don't see any sign of any bramble bushes.'

The dusty road in front of them was serene, timeless almost. She had always got a kick out of an open road. They must have walked an hour by now. She had felt a compulsion to walk tonight, as if she was tramping something undesirable into the ground with every step she took.

'Just along the road a bit. Where the proper countryside starts. Me and this girl skived school one day last year. It was really hot so we just walked around, went as far as we could. We ended up having a picnic. Brambles and cider and Mars Bars.'

Was it a whole year ago? School was already a blur. One day you were going to art school or going to be a singer — the next you were walking into the first place that would give you money. She remembered a narrow road between hedgerows, a road that had been there before the New Town. It had been a day similar to this, except hotter, with vertical lemon light painting black shadows around everything.

'How do you know they're still there?'

'Where are they going to go? Pull up their roots and walk away?'

'Another five minutes. Then we're heading back, right?'

They were overtaken by three boys on bikes. As soon as the boys were safely past they turned and shouted obscenities. She smiled wearily but he felt obliged to chase them for a few yards, trying to keep his can steady. He said: 'All I can see up ahead is another roundabout.'

She stood on tiptoe, one hand on his shoulder, and shaded her eyes.

'That wasn't there the last time,' she said uncertainly.

'Come on. We're going back. This is not my idea of how to spend a Friday night. We should have gone to Edinburgh like I said.'

'I want to find those bramble bushes.'

It had become imperative.

'They're long gone, sweetheart. Every time you blink around here another field's turned into a housing estate. Houses that you and me'll never be able to afford either.'

'Just a bit further.'

They went on as far as the roundabout he had indicated (surely the last one in the town?) but there was no likely hedgerow near it. Unwilling to give up, she tried two of its radial turn-offs but the flat fields spurned recognition.

'Your head's wasted. You said yourself you were on the cider.'

She shook her head in irritation.

'I'm heading back,' he stated. 'Come on.'

'I want to find those bushes. It's bugging me.'

'Suit yourself. I'm going. I mean it.'

'Please.'

'It's getting late. I want to hear some music.'

As he walked away, she knew that he was waiting for her to trail after him, could see it in the confident swagger of his shoulders. She stood there thinking black thoughts, black, black . . .

But in a few moments he was out of sight and she knew that he would not wait for her now. Towards the town pink shale bings, coated thinly in grass like verdigris, shouldered their way above all the houses and the half-built Lego blocks of the industrial estates. The most distant bings she had grown up with, before the New Town had eaten up their village. Even then the bings had been monuments to a dead industry.

She listened to the steady click of her heels in the silence that had fallen with his leaving. Ankle boots with stilettos were hardly practical for long walks and these ones were designed for posing rather than using. She thought she could feel some chafing on her heels. She walked faster — a girl on her own — Friday night — hardly inconspicuous sexually either, she knew.

By the time she reached the next roundabout back towards the town centre she was slightly out of breath and the click-click of her boots was deafening. There was still no sign of him. Of the four roads radiating from the roundabout she tried the one on the right first, holding her head erect. Dead end. For future development. A few yards down the next one her attention was caught by a plastic strip, red and white diagonals, strung between two stakes.

Beyond the plastic strip was a narrow grey road with eroded verges. Between two hedgerows. She stopped herself from shouting on him just in time: she was on her own now. She had been right, though. This was the place.

She ducked underneath, glancing around first. The hedgerow to the left, on the town side, was a mosaic of brightness in the almost horizontal sunlight. A late butterfly flickered past, a windborne petal, and she could hear insects droning.

The brambles hung in purple clumps, pounds of them, with here and there a green-pink knot of hard unripened berries. She had forgotten about the tiny whiskers they had. Plucking one, two, a handful, she scanned them quickly for insects and then pushed them into her mouth. They were the purest fruit she had ever tasted, heady in the concentration of their flavour. She smiled as she ate them.

Foraging again, she felt her finger pricked. She had forgotten about the thorns too. There was a tiny bead of blood on her finger among the red juice stains. Much the same when it came down to it, she thought, sucking her finger.

Time contracted around her. She remembered days with jam jars, plastic bags, ferrying brambles back to her mother. Free fruit, the highlight of a day — though most of the stored berries ended up wasted, crushed together, left too long so that they turned into a furry blue fermentation.

Then she saw that she could be the last person ever to eat brambles from these bushes. Thirty yards ahead, the hedgerow and the road and the adjacent fields had all been ripped up and flattened, most of the grass clawed out by JCBs. A new, wider road was approaching, its rubble leaving an ebb point which would soon engulf this place.

She looked around her, feeling both sad and somehow fortunate, privileged even. Then suddenly she became self-conscious. If anyone she knew found her standing here like this. Time to go. The sunlight now only fringed the top of the hedgerow. On a whim she took a wad of violet tissue from her shoulder-bag and carefully wrapped a handful of the blackest fruit inside. Then she walked smartly back to the main road.

The blue FRESH VEG DA LY van pulled up with the driver's door slid back.

'Lift?'

'OK.' She went round to the other side.

'Had a row with the boyfriend?'

She shrugged. He was about five years older than her, maybe more, and had a black moustache.

'There he is now,' he remarked over the engine noise some minutes later. 'Want me to stop?'

The van slowed. He no longer had his can, was walking doggedly now. She waited for him to look back, willed it through the dusty windscreen — though the will was already half-hearted. He did not turn round, however, and she said with finality: 'No.'

She did not look back either.

NOTES ON CONTRIBUTORS

BALFOUR BROWN   Born Greenock 1924. Poems, mainly in *London Magazine*. Contributor to *Scottish Short Stories* (Collins).

ELIZABETH BURNS   Lives in Edinburgh and works as a publisher. Her poetry has appeared in magazines and in anthologies including *Original Prints* and the Third Eye Centre's *Behind the Lines*.

STEWART CONN   Born Glasgow 1936. Now lives in Edinburgh. Married with two sons. Poems anthologised in *A Sense of Belonging, Noise and Smoky Breath, Twelve More Modern Scottish Poets, The Best of Scottish Poetry*, and *NWS* 6. His most recent volume is *In the Kibble Palace* (Bloodaxe, 1987).

ROBERT CRAWFORD   Born Bellshill 1959, grew up in Glasgow, studied and taught English at Glasgow and Oxford, and is lecturer in Modern Scottish Literature at St Andrew's University. Co-editor of *Verse*, he wrote a book on T.S. Eliot, and has a selection of poems in *New Chatto Poets II* (1989).

LESLIE CROOK   Born Preston 1959. Resident in Glasgow. Plays — adaptations of Dickens, Molière and Plantins, and a satire 'The Misanthrope Amended'. Recently completed a Phaedra.

JOHN CUNNINGHAM   Born Edinburgh 1934, farmed in Galloway for about twenty-five years, now living in Glasgow. Stories published in various magazines, including *West Coast Magazine* and in the 1989 Collins collection of short stories *The Red Hog of Colima*.

ELSPETH DAVIE   Born Ayrshire, spent early years in south of England. School, University and College of Art in Edinburgh. Taught painting for some years. Married, with one daughter, lived for a time in Ireland before returning to

Scotland. Four collections of short stories. Four novels, the latest *Coming to Light* (Hamish Hamilton, 1989).

G.F. DUTTON   Born 1924 of Anglo-Scottish parentage. Travelled much of the globe, most of life in Scotland. Publications from enzymology to mountaineering. First collection of poems, *Camp One* (Macdonald, 1978) won SAC New Writing Award, second collection *Squaring the Waves* (Bloodaxe, 1986), SAC Book Award. His third collection of verse *The Concrete Garden* will also be published by Bloodaxe.

GERRIE FELLOWS   Born New Zealand 1954. Childhood spent there and in London. Has lived in Glasgow since 1983. Her poetry is published in a number of journals and in anthologies from Stramullion (*Fresh Oceans*) and Polygon (*Original Prints III*). A collection of poetry, *Technologies*, is forthcoming from Polygon.

ALEXANDER FENTON   Born 1929, brought up in Drumblane and Auchterless, Aberdeenshire. Aberdeen and Cambridge Universities. Books and articles on Scottish country life. Worked on the *Scottish National Dictionary* then in the National Museum of Antiquities of Scotland and the National Museums of Scotland. Director, European Ethnological Research Centre.

RAYMOND FRIEL   Born Greenock 1963. Educated at St Mary's, Blairs, Aberdeen; St Patrick's College, Thurles, Eire and at Glasgow University. Currently reading for an M.Litt. in the poetry of W.H. Auden at Oxford University. Previous work published in *NWS 5*.

ROBIN FULTON   Born 1937, has lived in Norway since 1973. His latest translations include Tomas Transtromer's *Collected Poems* (Bloodaxe, 1987) and Par Lagerkvist's *Quests of Reality* (Quartet, 1989). His *The Way the Words are Taken* (Macdonald, 1989) is a selection of essays and reviews.

JANICE GALLOWAY   Born in Ayrshire though now lives in Glasgow. Short stories published in every major Scottish literary magazine and anthologies from Polygon, Women's Press, Serpent's Tail, BBC etc. Recently completed a stage adaptation of Radclyffe Hall's *The Wall of Loneliness*. *The Trick is to Keep Breathing* (first novel) will be published by Polygon this year.

MICHAEL GARDINER   Born Ayr 1970. Has spent time working and living in Ayr and Glasgow, and travelling in the USA. Will read English at the University of Oxford, beginning October 1989. Currently lives in Glasgow.

WILLIAM GILFEDDER   Born Glasgow 1945. Left school at fifteen with no qualifications. Various jobs: van boy, apprentice motor mechanic, driver; at present works as a gardener/handyman. Poems published in *Scottish Review*, *The Glasgow Magazine* and *NWS* 5.

JOHN GLENDAY   Born Broughty Ferry 1952. Lives in Carnoustie and works as a psychiatric nurse in Dundee. First collection of poetry *The Apple Ghost* published by Peterloo Poets in May 1989. Poems in various magazines and anthologies including *Chapman*, *The Fiddlehead*, *NWS* 6, *Times Literary Supplement* and *The Wascana Review*.

RODERICK HART   Born Aberdeenshire 1944, but grew up in St Andrews. A graduate of Aberdeen University, he is now a lecturer at Telford College, Edinburgh. His work has previously appeared in magazines, *The Scotsman* and four anthologies of Scottish writing.

W.N. HERBERT   Born Dundee 1961 and educated locally and at Brasenose College, Oxford, where he is currently completing a thesis on Hugh MacDiarmid. He has published two pamphlets of Scots verse, *Sterts and Stobies* and *Severe Burns*, and is compiling a volume called *Poems in English*.

RICHARD JACKSON   Born Galashiels 1937. Read at Royal High School (with Hector MacIvor) and St Andrews University. Taught English for ten years. Turned gamekeeper for HM Inspectorate of Schools and Colleges. Became mainline administrator in arts and libraries; social work; prisons; primary health care. Sings; acts; sometimes writes.

ROBERT ALAN JAMIESON   Born Shetland 1958. Author of novels *Soor Hearts* and *Thin Health*; a collection of poetry

Shoormal; a Shetlandic play *An Aald Lion Lies Doon*. Originated *Briggistanes*, a creative writing broadsheet based in Shetland. Collaborated with composer David Ward on a cantata *Beyond the Far Haaf*, to be premiered in 1990. Currently finishing a new novel.

DAVID KINLOCH   Born Lennoxtown 1959. Graduated Glasgow University 1982. Since then has studied in Oxford and Paris. Until recently a Fellow of the University of Wales, he now works in Manchester as lecturer in French at the University of Salford. Is a co-editor of *Verse*. Work published in *NWS* 1,2, 3, 5 and 6. Work forthcoming in *London Magazine*.

BOB LAST   Born 1955. Educated England, New Zealand, USA, Scotland. Lived in Edinburgh since 1970. Businessman.

MAURICE LINDSAY   Born Glasgow 1918. Sixteen books of poems, most recently, *Requiem for a Sexual Athlete*. Other books include *The Burns Encyclopedia*, *History of Scottish Literature*, *The Castles of Scotland*, most recently, the paperback *Glasgow*. Anthologies include *Modern Scottish Poetry*, *An Anthology of the Scottish Renaissance*, *A Book of Scottish Verse* (with R.L. Mackie) and most recently in paperback, *Scotland: An Anthology*. Has been programme controller, Border Television, Director, the Scottish Civic Trust and is now Honorary Secretary-General, Europe Nostra and President, the Association for Scottish Literary Studies.

PETER McCAREY   Born Paisley 1956, now translating in Geneva for WHO. Author of *Hugh MacDiarmid and the Russians* (Scottish Academic Press, 1988) and co-author of *For What It Is* (Christchurch NZ, Untold Press, 1988).

KENNETH MacDONALD   Born Paisley 1959. Work published in *NWS* 5 and 6. Has recently completed first novel, a cheesy detective yarn set in Glasgow and Paisley. When not writing, cheering on Motherwell FC, or listening to Loudon Wainwright III records, can usually be found trying to talk wife into yet another American holiday.

JAMES McGONIGAL   Born Dumfries 1947. Now lives in Cumbernauld New Town. Teacher, father, occasional writer and researcher, and lay Dominican. *Unidentified Flying Poems* (1981). Recent poetry in *Temenos, New Blackfriars* and *NWS* 6. Currently producing an anthology: *Almighty Rows/Infernal Arguments.*

ALISTAIR MACKIE   Born Aberdeen 1925. Graduated with Honours in English from Aberdeen University 1950. Began writing in Scots in 1954. Three publications in Scots, *Clytach* (Akros), *Back-green Odyssey* (Rainbow Books), and *Ingaitherins* (AUP). Retired from teaching in 1983. Work appearing in forthcoming *European Translations in Scots* (EUP).

HUGH McMILLAN   Born Dumfries 1955. Educated Dumfries Academy and Edinburgh University. Recent poems in *Lines Review, Poetry Australia, Poetry Review, The Listener.* First small collection *Too Much Insalata* (Envoi). Awarded SAC Writers' Bursary 1988/89.

GORDON MEADE   Born Perth 1957. Lives in East Neuk of Fife. Poems in many magazines including *Blind Serpent, Cencrastus, Chapman, The Glasgow Magazine, Lines Review, Radical Scotland* and *Understanding.* Poems in *NWS* 5 and 6. Read at 1989 Mayfest New Poets and at ASLS AGM. Currently preparing a reading for STV's In Verse.

JAMES MEEK   Born London 1962. School in Dundee, university in Edinburgh and London. Novel *McFarlane Boils the Sea* published 1989. Currently employed as a newspaper reporter in Edinburgh, where he lives.

W.S. MILNE   Born Aberdeen 1953. Educated Portlethen, Dyce and Bankhead. Degrees in English, University of Newcastle upon Tyne. Lived and worked in London area for the past seven years. Poems in various magazines, including *Cencrastus, Chapman, Lallans* and *Lines Review.*

MICHAEL MUNRO   Born Glasgow 1954. Works as a publisher's editor. Author of two books on Glasgow dialect: *The Patter* (GDL, 1985), and *The Patter — Another Blast* (Canongate, 1987). Short stories in *NWS* 4 and 6, *The Glasgow Herald, The Scottish Cat* (AUP), *Streets of Gold* (Mainstream). Occasional poems in various magazines.

THOM NAIRN   Born Perthshire 1955, managing editor of *Cencrastus* and a co-editor of *SLJ Review Supplement*. Currently completing PhD on Sydney Goodsir Smith. Poetry and criticism in various magazines and anthologies: *NWS* 5 and 6, *Chapman*, *Rialto*, *Poetry Wales* etc. Work also recorded for STV's In Verse series.

WILLIAM NEILL   Born 1922. Educated Ayr Academy, Edinburgh University. Eight collections of verse (Gaelic, Scots, English), latest *Wild Places*, *Making Tracks*. SAC Book Award 1985. Poetry broadcasts for Radio Scotland, STV. Former editor of *Catalyst* and *Lallans*. Lives in Galloway.

DONNY O'ROURKE   Born Port Glasgow 1959. Educated St Mirin's Academy, Paisley, and Glasgow University. Poems in *Cencrastus*, *Lines*, *Radical Scotland*, *West Coast* and broadcast on BBC Radio Scotland. Arts producer with Scottish Television. Writes on folk music for *Glasgow Herald*, *New Statesman* and other journals.

RICHARD PRICE   Born England 1966. Degree in English and Librarianship, University of Strathclyde. Works in the British Library. Poems in *The Glasgow Herald*, *Cencrastus*, and *The Scottish Dog*. Currently researching the fiction of Neil Gunn for a forthcoming EUP book.

J.N. REILLY   Born Glasgow 1957. Work in *Edinburgh Review* 78/9, *West Coast Magazine* 2, 3, 4, *NWS* 6 and the anthologies *Workers City* and *Behind the Lines*. The author of seven books currently awaiting an enlightened publisher, he is, amongst other projects, currently translating the complete works of Arthur Rimbaud.

ALAN RIACH   Born Lanarkshire 1957. Degrees from Cambridge and Glasgow, Fellow of Waikato University, Hamilton, New Zealand. Work has appeared in numerous journals in Scotland, NZ and Australia, including *NWS* 5 and 6. *For What It Is*, written with Peter McCarey, is published by Untold Books, Christchurch, NZ. Auckland University Press are to publish his poems 1978-88.

IAIN ROBERTSON SCOTT   Born Falkirk 1954. Highland/ Lowland background. PhD from Edinburgh University on the politics of Wordsworth and Coleridge. Teacher of history in Edinburgh. Has written on Romanticism in *Britain and the French Revolution* (Macmillan, 1989). Currently completing a book on his favourite place, *Discovering Skye*. 'The Helmet' is his first work of fiction.

JENNY TURNER   Born Aberdeen, 1963. Came to Edinburgh for university in 1980 and still lives there.

ISABELLA M. WALKER   Born at Dowies Mill, near Auld Cramond Brig 1934. Graduated MA (Hons) History of Art, Edinburgh University 1984. Cutrently to be found frequenting antiquarian bookshops pursuing new interest in illustrated books or wandering about the countryside delighting in wild flowers. Poetry published in *NWS* 5 and 6.

BILL WATT   Born Greenock 1950. Received a First in English from Stirling University and is presently teaching in Broxburn Academy, West Lothian. Started writing poetry this past year, though long fiction is represented by Maclean Dubois (Writers and Agents) of Edinburgh.